·PORTRAITS·

ALSO BY DANIEL BERRIGAN

PROSE
The Bride: Essays in the Church
The Bow in the Clouds
Consequences; Truth And
Love, Love at the End
They Call Us Dead Men
Night Flight to Hanoi
No Bars to Manhood
The Dark Night of Resistance
America is Hard to Find
The Geography of Faith (with Robert Coles)
Absurd Convictions, Modest Hopes (with Lee Lockwood)
Jesus Christ
Lights on in the House of the Dead
The Raft Is Not the Shore (with Nhat Hanh)
A Book of Parables
Uncommon Prayer: A Book of Psalms
Beside the Sea of Glass: The Song of the Lamb
The Words Our Savior Gave Us
The Discipline of the Mountain
We Die Before We Live
Ten Commandments for the Long Haul

POETRY
Time Without Number
No One Walks Waters
Encounters
The World for Wedding Ring
False Gods, Real Men
Trial Poems (with Tom Lewis)
Prison Poems
Selected and New Poems

DRAMA
Trial of the Catonsville Nine

·PORTRAITS·

Of Those I Love

DANIEL BERRIGAN

CROSSROAD · NEW YORK

1984

The Crossroad Publishing Company
370 Lexington Avenue, New York, N.Y. 10017

Printed in the United States of America

Library of Congress Cataloging in Publication Data

Berrigan, Daniel.
Portraits—of those I love.

I. Title.
PS3503.E734P6   818'.5403   [B]   81-17490
ISBN 0-8245-0482-8   ISBN 0-8245-0416-X pbk.   AACR2

CONTENTS

To Jim and Rosalie
late but with love.

PREFACE

This book is envisioned as a tribute to friendship.

Friendship: a tame subject indeed, not rating high on any Richter Scale of Crucial Topics I know of. It is nonetheless, as grandiloquent Cicero, along with the Greeks, Bacon, La Rochefoucauld, and Montaigne have reminded us, "a gentle and universal warmth, moderate and even."

If I may more narrowly regard my subject, friendship is also a chief delight of the celibate life. This in a strange time, ours, when more intense initiatives so often perish at birth of contending fevers and chills—die perhaps, of too much, too quickly.

A time, moreover, when immodest claims are raised in regard to something called sexuality, an item peddled indeed far, wide, and handsomely, not merely about the seedy Times Squares of this world, but even door to door—yours and mine.

In this enterprise, we are seriously assured, such things as technique and performance are worthy of the dizzy status of human credentials.

More, purportedly serious tomes pile up in religious stalls, instructing the benighted celibate that *this* cake can be both had and eaten.

All of which evokes in me a certain wry memory.

When I dwelt at Cornell in the late sixties, it was a dogma as rigid as any held by a strong-arm church that hip folk of both sexes shacked up. Simple as that. The rules allowed for no other arrangement. If you were someone referred to as a "movement person," you had one or more sexual connections. The venture might be transient, quasi permanent, ensconced in marriage, or a matter of broken-field bed hopping. (Faculty arrangements were another game, often in the Cheever mode of undercover partner swapping and weekend safaris. No high-minded prof, need it be said, ever referred to such things with so ungentle a term as *adultery.*)

As I recall, religious folk, and especially Catholics, tended to take second looks at all this, looks from skeptical to scandalous. Someone like myself, who was known to keep bachelor's digs, to move in a wide circle of the third estate, and moreover, qualified in the antiwar movement, was regarded variously with amusement or puzzlement. Ivy-League rules, as well as the early SDS code, forbade intemperate probing. But now and again, the question would surface face to face (as it was surely an intriguing topic about campus): "What's this type all about? You mean he actually doesn't go to bed with *anyone?*"

Well, actually, he didn't.

Another episode casts a measure of light on those times.

I departed Cornell under somewhat bizarre circumstances, which need not detain us here. The FBI, prompt as taxes and death, came round. Their prey had evaded them—but perhaps he had left a spoor? The point of their probing about was to discover whether I might have left behind some trace, faint or noisome, of sexual goings-on. In the peculiar ethic of that fraternity, such evidence could be usefully applied to taint the Matter of the Catonsville Nine, then before the courts.

Alas, those fervent hounds came on exactly nothing.

But as to the matter of this book.

I regard *friendship* as a canopy word, under which those I love and write of here, living or departed, may, so to speak, rest assured.

It may seem strange that under this rubric I recall my own mother, dead these several years. Yet toward the end of her life, when illness brought her low, and multiplied blows had brought me to a different mind, this is exactly what we became: friends. It may have been the imminence of death, prison endured or in prospect, the tragedy of times we so barely survived. Half-blind, hardly able to lift a hand, she would stroke my face and murmur, "My joy, you are my joy." All that old-time religion, that pride of priesthood, of mother of the priest, was vanished. Life the leveler, so skilled in breaking the back of ego, healed even as it wounded. We looked in one another's eyes and saw something better than pride of place: life giving, a conquest. Down, dog death!

My mother's story may help explain my treatment of other friendships recorded here. My aunt was another unlikely friend to such as me; she in her last years, I without a gray hair to comb. More, when we met periodically, noblesse oblige put me on the listening and learning end of the log. Thus, the classical requirements of friendship, mutuality and equality, were lacking to us. No matter; a simple fact restored all. For I loved this old, plucky woman in her worn shoes and enveloping shroud, her phosphorescent mind casting sparks around. Visiting her was no Irish penance; she simply delighted and intrigued.

To meet her, I think, was to encounter something called in our family lexicon "the verities"—all old-fashioned, not one of them poisoned with chic or cheap relevance. Through her, I think, my brothers and I fed our suspicion (more than a suspicion, a conviction eventually felonious, indictable) that something was rotten, in someplace other than Denmark.

Peter Maurin I never met, a circumstance that may appear inhibiting to friendship. Until it is recalled that most of us have yet to pass a time of incubating love with various admired mentors, peers, gurus, saviors, opposite numbers. Something still awaits, we are promised, under another sky, and we in a more serviceable frame than "the body of this death."

Until that happy hour, we are told to be vigilant, to cling, in the teeth of the mad times, to an absurd hope. To make do, in sum (as occurs in the matter of Peter and myself), with whatever memories, hints, emblems, episodes make up the oral and written tradition of friends of friends. In my life, this secondary arrangement has been of value; Dorothy Day and her circle of Catholic Workers drew me to Peter. In suchwise, the living and the dead conspired; and I was hooked.

Of the others who inhabit these pages, John McNeil may stand surrogate for a number of Jesuits of my generation who have redeemed, in a thin time, the order and its works and pomps. Redeemed, in this minimal and obscure sense: that they helped me bear with what things would not, or could not, be changed or evangelized or cleansed. The temple worship goes on, as does the worship of money, power, distraction from the holy and lowly.

Still there are friends, who redeem the times.

A redeeming friendship? It seems to me a very old idea, which a deadly era and a worse culture conspire to make new.

In my early years in the order, warnings aplenty were scattered about, like handfuls of blue nails, to make jagged the path of friendship. Something, oxymoronic or tautological, I know not which, was darkly referred to as "particular friendship."

We were to learn, as our education proceeded, of the existence of another barrier against mutuality, what may be called rules of exclusion. These were defined in canon law, or promulgated in accord with curial pleasure or angst. Among these rules were those enumerating certain forbidden topics or areas of research or modes of conduct long since condemned. Above this turf, a shingle was hung. Its legend: Private Property: Keep Off.

Some of us have learned a few things: that friendship in the nature of things human or divine tends to the particular. Those who leaped the first barrier then made a further discovery: Certain canonical prohibitions, implicit or clearly spelled out, which excluded women, gays, others, from the common table or font or anointing, were as inhuman and spiritually destructive as the earlier "thou shalt nots" aimed at the heart of our youth.

It was at this second barrier that I met John McNeil.

In the middle sixties, I had been tossed about boisterously in the grab bag of fortune for daring to surmise aloud that the

Vietnam war was not exactly America's or Christianity's finest hour. Years later, along came John. He was employed, so to speak, in applying a lever against the lid of a can of dark and living surmises. And for this, it was decreed, he was to be tossed to oblivion, likewise. Thus, two soldiers of misfortune met; the friendship goes on, trouble and redemption in uneasy passage.

Of Dorothy Day and Christina and Thomas Merton, little need be said here. When their faces arise in my mind, life stops in its tracks. Old loss or fresh, it makes little difference; it is the loss that exacts and hurts.

And yet I reflect, for every loss a dark gain. A better argument could not be devised for the eternity of our substance than the ache, which is unhealable in this life, for lost friends. The theme runs through pagan and Christian classics: Friendship is a guarantor of eternity, however construed.

How eternity is to be construed, Christians, at least, can have little doubt. In losing a friend to death, Augustine wrote, he lost the half of his soul. But he went on to assure himself, and us, that if the half is lost, we shall regain the whole.

With this book, I summon my dear friends Dorothy, Christina, Thomas, Peter, my mother, Josephine. Against death the omnipresent, the omnivorous, the would-be omnipotent; whether death's misbegotten misnomer be neutron bomb, or betrayal of Christian by Christian, or acedia of spirit, or the refusals and reprisals that jar our soul off course—against fealty to these, or complicity in these, my friends place a hand over my mouth, an exorcising hand on my brow.

Fear not. You shall see our face.

·1·
THE MONK

Well over a decade ago, the long sea trek of Thomas Merton culminated in his death in Bangkok. The facts of his death are so simple, so well known. Yet even at this long remove, they stop the heart in its tracks. Everyone knows how he died; a decade later, who can resign himself to such a death? Who has gotten used to his absence? We bear it because we must.

We were not sure, when he set out across country and into the East, what he was thinking—especially about us (the "us" in this case being the nine who in May of 1968 invaded the draft board at Catonsville, Maryland, and burned draft files). How did Merton take all that? The question was on all our minds. That summer, he wrote a kind of reaction in a Catholic weekly, *Ave Maria*. The clearest impression I have of his mood is a mix of alertness and bewilderment. He was stirred, fearful, didn't know where such acts might lead. He trusted us, but his trust was tested hard. In any case, he seemed to need more time to make up his mind.

We had been through this before. Tragedies, new directions connected with the war, set him rocking. Isolated as he was, he had no chance to be in on the sweat, discussion, prayer that went into an act like Catonsville. And when catastrophe struck, as in the case of the self-immolation of Roger Laporte at the

United Nations in 1965, he tended to panic. One or another of us would thereupon go down to the monastery to help put things in focus. He simmered down, thought things over, and went on with us, at his own measured pace.

But after Catonsville, from May to December of 1968, there were no more visits to the monastery. I don't remember quite why, except that neither side pushed for a meeting. I can only record the impression that he was tired, fed up with a war that seemed to go on forever, that had no sense, no outcome. More, Merton was finding that even the solitude of his Kentucky eyrie was not immune against crazies. They kept coming around, like crows to a feeding station.

Then a breakthrough. A new abbot was elected at Gethsemane. Merton's hopes, deferred for years, welled up. He planned a pilgrimage into the world, some twenty-five years after he had left it, on a new basis indeed, seeking out a possible place for himself, a new setting.

His life had been a long patience, a long loneliness. There is no point in going over once again all he had suffered during the monastic years. The story has been told in part; someone will tell it more completely in good time. When the news came that he was setting out, we rejoiced because his hopes, so long put off, so arbitrarily squelched, were about to spring. One phase was over; it had seemed at times like the fate of those stuck at the base of Dante's original seven-story mountain:

> *colui che mostra se piu negligente*
> *che se pigrizia fosse sua serocchia . . .*

Always with the difference, of course, that Merton had put in his time, not as a time server, but simply as a patient, hard-wrung, gracious monk, a kind of long-distance runner in place, a master of hangman's humor. And to me, a friend peerless among friends, a gift given once or twice in a lifetime.

We had endured a few things together. There were crises and good times on both sides, things to laugh and weep about. The late fifties and the sixties plunged us into a scene where sanity at times looked like madness, where the highest art possible to the artful was simply hanging on.

In his case, the art followed the old classical norm: It hid itself well. To the world at large, he was the immensely productive author, book upon book, a large audience assured. He had the industry of a beehive, the discipline. More, he had a mandate from the community: "Keep at it." The scope of his interests grew apace; he began to take seriously the world he had shrunk from with the fastidiousness of the new convert. At first, that world had seemed manifestly bad; then gradually (maybe because he met specimens like us, hot from the hot spot), not so bad. Then the facade of fallen hopes, fallen loves, fallen kingdoms—it fell away. The world showed him its tragic bloodshot face.

By then he was getting somewhere.

I mean on his own terms, as he came to understand them: a monk, a man of prayer, a worldly man on the qui vive, a recluse for the kingdom's sake, a lucid, cutting mind that in a hundred ways helped us stand somewhere, mainly by standing with us. In entering the monastery, he had taken a large step backward from our world, a tactic the French proverb commends "in order to leap further." The leap was not long in coming, a mighty one indeed, a world record.

He leapt, and yet he stayed put. Rumors came and went; he was leaving the monastery, he was gone, he had returned to New York, he had left the church. It was all slightly dotty, or more than slightly; malice lurked in some of it. But such effluvia meant little to him; he issued a good-humored denial of this or that account of purported backsliding and kept plugging away at his own life. He was moving into more responsibility, an elder by now, in charge of the novices of the community.

By and large, the early sixties were good times. He brought people of all kinds to the monastery; his spirit was ecumenical; now he had scope to try out his instincts. Protestant seminarians came from Louisville; a rabbi from Canada; Catholics such as Philip, myself, many others. Merton wanted the young monks to learn something of the currents then riding fiercely across the church and the world. As usual, he put things bluntly: There would be no monastic prayer worth talking about without such exposure, grounding. One noticed changes in the novitiate—

vitality, good art, good books, clippings from newspapers. It was worlds apart from the musty sacristy religion that would drive even a mouse berserk with boredom. Dignity, lucidity, gracefulness, clean air—I remember it well, with a pang. And I wonder about the pang those young monks must feel now, years after, wherever life has borne them.

I forget time and years; it must have been around 1965 that he brought friends together for a retreat. (Gordon Zahn wrote of it at some length in *Another Part of the War,* published in 1979.) Some ten or twelve of us were invited to discuss and pray together, according to his suggestion, on the subject "roots of protest." There was a Mennonite theologian, an aged revered minister (he ought to be invoked rather than named: A. J. Muste, pray for us), Catholic Workers, a friend from Hutchins's Center for the Study of Democratic Institutions in Santa Barbara, a few priests, my brother Phil, myself. Those two or three days have, in retrospect, the charged aura of a myth; practically all who took part have by now either died or undergone prison.

One delicious episode stays with me. Philip and another priest had arrived late. As things transpired, a liturgy had been proposed; it was to be ecumenical—but within limits. Merton passed the word to us Catholics: By instruction of the abbot, only we were allowed to take communion. (What seems barbarous now was then fairly standard practice. The separated brethren [sic] were still being "separated out," a quite active verb for Catholics.) We agreed. In fact there was nothing else to do; we were guests. Besides, the prohibition was no great departure from standard discourtesy. In any case, Philip careened in, just as communion was under way. Not having had the law read to him, and burdened with few native inhibitions, he simply passed the communion to whomever was in his vicinity. In the vicinity of course were several Protestants. They took communion. *Sic solvitur.* One of them said to me later, "If only I had known things were so simple! What are we waiting for?"

On another occasion, a Baptist minister and I visited Merton. On the way to the monastery, he told me of a nightmare he had sweated through the night before. He dreamed he was at the monastery chapel, taking part in a Catholic mass. Shock, cold

sweat indeed. We arrived at the monastery somewhat late in the
evening and were shown to rooms. The next morning, when
Merton came to greet us, he proposed that we take part in the
community liturgy. A "Catholic mass" if ever there was one! I
stole a sidelong look at my friend; his eyes held a look seldom
seen on land or sea. Merton had that way with him—face the
incubus, exorcise it. *Sic solvitur* . . .

I remember him as quintessentially a modern man to his
fingertips: his slang, his ironies, the bravery that kept him on the
move, his skepticism about big claims and names, his mind's cat
prowl in the long night of the world, his skill at putting a finger
on a sore spot, an illusion, a put-on. He was a monk; he was in
touch. He was never, not for a moment, *relevant* or *efficient*, those
catch basins for waste and want. Indeed, he would shoot fire
when such words came up, on monastic lips or others. He met
phoniness in high places with a barely controlled fury whose
second phase on good days was hilarity and mockery. On bad
days, there was no second phase. Then he simply lived with
what he was forced to, knowing bad days do not last forever.

He was complex; but he was more than a grab bag of great
talents. Complexity went deeper; he had lived several avatars
before the monastery years, was instructed in the mad modern
dance, which had spun him through Europe and New York,
through marxism, hedonism, agnosticism, into church and
monastery. Integrating all that into a life of personal truthfulness, sanity, could not be easy. There always shone through the
radiant, disciplined face that subdued soul light.

He hadn't, to change the image, gotten found by leaving a
trail of debris behind. He brought along on the mountain of
purgation every bone conviction, love unfeigned, courtesy, a
sardonic sidelong glance. It took years I think, before he could
trust himself to be himself, something perhaps usual in tumultu-
ous converts. Then in the last years, everything came together;
he was engaging, noncombative, listening, graceful, utterly
warm of heart, even naive and gentle. He had no fetishes; he had
nothing but the truth to defend, and that was a light burden. I
remember his soul force, in the Gandhian sense, his strength,
the plain talk you could expect from him. When he saw some-

thing, he said what he saw and stood by it. And he expected the same of his friends, that we would pay up.

What life exacted of him there is no need of totting up here. For perhaps the final ten years, tragedy entered his life. Severe limits were put on his writing and publishing; he was censored, reproved, forbidden to write on nuclear arms or modern war. He began to see the contradictions and follies that make ecclesiastical structures into secular traps. He was denied half of his soul, that half that was newly afire with the mad truth of the times: that the times were death ridden, that the society was hell-bent on a suicide run. He saw it, and he could not say it. A new vocation was flowering in the shell of the old: peacemaking. They said nay, they blessed their nay. And the act drew blood.

There was a kind of crazy consonance to all this. It was the mid sixties; if you were in the church, in his circumstances, it made sense (so we were preached to also) to make no sense. Blood was being shed in prodigious draughts by Americans, the Draculas of war. Some few thought it was time, past time, to staunch the flow, given the skills of healing that the church was purportedly in possession of. Nothing of the kind, or better, for a very long time, a time of random, needless death, very little of the kind. In my case, the big guns of obedience were wheeled out, wondrous statements were uttered as to the inadmissibility of serious action. Like this one: "Such actions [as Catonsville] are Christian; they are not however Jesuit." Things could hardly have been put more damningly by the worst traducer of the order.

Merton's case was roughly parallel. Juggernaut and judgment, the war went on; it was declared off limits to the conscience of monk and Jesuit. The monks' role was prayer; mine was—what? Anything, as long as it remained ineffectual, law-abiding. (Gospel-abiding? The question seldom arose.)

It was the law, not the war, that threatened to destroy us both. The irony once stated (an irony I find almost unbearable even today), one can leave it at that. The law did not destroy him or me. We survived the law, including the law of the church. Whether the law should ever have been invoked, whether its invocation was not rather an incanting of the gods of war, or whether, on the other hand, his order and mine should have encouraged and blessed our work, our attempt at being faithful (peacemaking instead of complicity)—these are painful matters indeed. Today it must be added that such matters remain largely unresolved in the church, as indeed they are unresolved in the secular kingdom of the blind. They hover on the air, a nuke of Damocles. What was unlearned (better, plain rejected) in the sixties is still rejected. The brave protests of Popes John and Paul against nuclear adventuring and genocidal tradeoffs—these cries wander like landless doves over the flood, return without relief to the beleaguered ark.

Still my friend suffered and did what he could, kept messages coming, stuffing them in bottles and casting them on the tide. He never gave up; he stayed put. If he cried Armageddon, he did so largely in the teeth of a wind that all but knocked him flat. His was, I think, the purest kind of truth telling, the kind that endures even in the empire of the deaf.

My mind returns often to this—he stayed put. It was not that he hid out, or vegetated, or gave up, or joined the officers' club, or hardened, or softened, or shrugged away his plight or ours. It meant that he had a place, a center, convictions that held, a sense of himself, wary and troubled as he was.

He reminds me of one of the Vietnamese Buddhist monks he so loved and learned from: Say, a monk of Hué dragging his altar into the streets and sitting down there to protest the mad war. The tanks arrive; the monk stays put. Because the monk stays put, the tank is confounded. What does a tank do when a monk refuses to "move when so ordered"? The tank has choices, but they are not large. Can we imagine a tank rubbing its iron skull in puzzlement before the immovable monk? The "it" has met the "he." It is a confrontation worth pondering; the implications are both millenial and hotly contemporary.

The impasse comes to this: The monk is more ready to die than the tank is to kill. And that is the rub indeed, for the tank is built to kill, only to kill. But the monk is not "built" at all, in order to do anything at all. If he is "for" anything, if he serves any purpose, if he has any goal in life, it quite surpasses the understanding of the tank (which is not quite equal to the prognostications of, say, a think tank). Indeed, the monk would also rub his skull in bewilderment at talk of "goals," "efficiency." For he serves no purpose, he has no goals, he is not "for" anything.

If he were to put the matter in words (and that also is unlikely), the monk might say something like this: He is called to be a pure and truthful expression of life itself. Of life. To be. Neither to strive, to gain, to lose, to earn, to spend, to be skilled, to be a pro, to ideologize, to make a mark, to be honored, to be dishonored, to survive, to perish. . . . It is all beside the point. The words befit the iron tread, the steely skull of the tank; they are not the words of a monk at all. Indeed, the words could imply a profound spiritual malaise, jaundice, disenchantment, disarray, even violence, thirst for blood. They imply a "come hither" to the tank. They offer a clue as to why tanks are thought necessary, are assembled, move in packs, why they do so well what tanks are made to do: kill.

But what has all this, this charade of force, this huff and puff, to do with the monk? He has something else to do: to stay put, to be. Especially to be, in places and times where life itself (his gift, his only love, his bride)—where life is endangered, put to naught, despised, obliterated. Then, oh, then he knows what must be done, he does what must be done!

And at that point something akin to the miraculous occurs. This solitary, foolish, exotic one, this silent refuser, this stubborn sitter, brings something to pass. Alive or dead, he brings it to pass. It being a matter of supreme indifference to him whether the tank stops short of him or rolls over him. He brings something to pass. He does something no other can do, because he stays put when all prudence, all legitimate self-interest, all logic, all casuistry unite in crying, in warning, "GET UP, MOVE IT, GET THE HELL OUT, THE TANKS ARE COMING!"

No, he stays put. He knows what he knows. What he knows is, he is called to stay put—an ecological rightness, nice to the hair's breadth—there in the path of the tank. This is his native ground; dangerous, they cry, they warn, flat out uninhabitable. No matter; where he belongs.

What does the monk offer us—the future, the unborn, the jaded, fed-up resisters, the makers and drivers of tanks? All of us, that is, whose destiny in one way or another converges on this unlikely distant scene: the tank and the monk? Who will prevail? Shall mere flesh and blood prevail? Shall spirit prevail? Shall death be robbed of its victory, its sting?

We long to know. I think the monk knows.

The Monk's Poems*

There is, first of all, the gargantuan size of this collection. Zounds! It compares impressively with the Works and Pomps of Any Giant of Literature You Care to Name; the avoirdupois of a complete Shakespeare, a complete Chaucer, a complete Bible.

Something like an elephant before one, eye to eye. Opening it is like climbing aboard.

In the age of *Jaws, Coma, The Book of Lists,* and "Haldeman's Hartifice," the book is indeed an astonishing event. A complete Merton, toe to topknot; so exhaustive, from juvenilia to his last breath, that the uninitiated might wonder if the man ever broke down and gave out with a bit of prose. Surely someone with a big clout loved Merton to bring this off.

He was set so firmly in my life that a review of his poems has the mournful aspect of an obituary, years after the fact. Is a book like this a delayed burial service, or a resurrection? Maybe something of both. The life is over; the myth takes shape.

But he was a myth, too, in our midst. Because he lived his life at some distance from our chills and fevers, even while he counted on us, and we on him. Esthetic distance? I think rather he saw his vocation as a necessary rehearsal, brought off in solitude, for that first big opening night. To do it well, death. To do it better than the culture could do it, or the culture-

*From *Collected Poems of Thomas Merton* (New York: New Directions, 1977).

ridden church. And his friends, and his enemies, and his community even, could take his resolve or leave it.

The poems were a relief he offered himself during the constant dog days, the prosaic days, that he chose to live. Plugging away, the long haul; what a workhorse he was! His relief was his friends, and his excursions into poetry, and his rhapsodic, fulminating, hilarious letters. These, and a bottle of beer on occasion. It was a monk's modest portion of this world. And he drank it all up.

Poetry: It is something like the age, which is to say, anything goes. The poets are children of this world; they bicker like crows and form into squads and schools like—poets. The motives are mixed, to say the least. They're hot after the returns, money, kudos. And the returns are diminishing. That makes for jaundice, infighting.

But Merton was apart from all that. He didn't need money; he didn't crave honor. If such came to him, that had a sort of mild interest; if they passed him by, that was okay too. So among the First Fifty Whooping Cranes, he could be called neither an academic poet, nor a confessional poet, nor a devotional poet. He never, in the wretched phrase, "plugged into" the latest fad or tic. As a result, he could breathe freely while he lived. And when he died, he paid the penalty—which was a sneering review of his poems in *The New York Times.*

I think he came closest to being a Buddhist poet, in the Chinese manner. The aura was the man; that is why, I think, his translations of Chuang are the best to be found. This was a spirit he could seize and run with, the tao. When I look for a hand grip on this slippery whale of a volume, I light with relief on these marvelous translations.

It was the way he lived! And he made it seem so effortless; he came on so lighthearted. He could write letters that were very jeremiads, verbal stonings of this or that idiocy. But in the flesh he was the tenderest and simplest of men. Toward the last years

I think he had crossed over; he could let go. It was the only valid way of holding on, firm. He had seized an irony that lies deep in the gospel, in Chinese Buddhism, in the lives of desert monks, in Gandhi, in his essays and conferences on Christ.

The tao: the unprogrammatic, unprovided for, unproven, uninitiated, unfettered way of the spirit. The discerning and embracing, a lover's embrace, the realities Paul celebrates—the things unseen. At the end Merton saw them, as *The Asian Journal* confesses.

There was another side of him: an iconoclast. False church, false faith, falsehood itself, he couldn't bear. But the image he railed loudest against was his own, the one they tried to saddle him with, whether celebrity or good, sheepish monk. I used to ask myself: Who taught him to be content with no one's opinion, base or flattering, of himself, his books, his fame, his following? The tao. Or as the testament has it, the Christ, who is also called the way.

Gratuity, grace. Life became an embolism of grace, life gathered around that reality, grace. He was a most giving man. And yet not at all a patsy, a victim, a parceled-out media freak. He had his center; it was cold as steel, warm as a heart. It had motion, rhythm, mobility; it was on its way—a tao.

Suppose someone who knew Merton and knew poetry were to cut the complete collection of his poems by nine of its tenths. The results might make this or that critic sit up and look alive. Still. The book as it stands is ironic, even hilarious. Merton would have guffawed at it; he would love it. Especially if he could give it away. And this is the spirit of the poetry too: a giveaway.

He took being a monk seriously. (That is why he could be so playful.) By serious I don't mean that he was narrow or cringing or kept scores. Somewhere, he had made up his mind. And no one could unmake it again. In consequence, he was a political man (the phrase would be understood by him as redundant). He included the sins and crimes of his century in his conscience, where they belonged, as elements of accountability. Such convictions colored his art as well.

All this made him a resister against the culture and got him in trouble inevitably. His order had a certain interest in peacekeeping, rather than in peacemaking. Moreover, like every order, his was not about to kowtow before one member, however presumably enlightened, publicly puffed, who was taking different soundings.

I hesitate to call this reaction to his rambunctiousness a superior wisdom or asceticism. There were other interests than conscience at stake (there always are): secular, even profane, like real estate, like the protection of the pecking order of authority. And more, a monastic male order is almost as vulnerable before *Roma Locuta* as an active order of women. Both are required, by every rule of the game, to keep things reasonably neat, their members in line. Both are presumed to be brick layers and water carriers for the Club of Rome. Or as one renowned monsignor orator reminded the Gethsemane community during a retreat, "You are the hidden violets, you are the unsigned cathedral masterpieces." No more inspired images could be devised for safeguarding the pyramid.

This galled Merton. It got into the poetry, whose accent at times was that of the underground, the beat.

He thought that a monk, at any given time, and emphatically in our time, ought to take his cues and style from, among others: blacks, women, homosexuals, welfare clients, Jews. This was a matter of right order, of history correctly grasped. The monk belonged at the edge. But unlike the other losers, he had no business fighting his way out toward respectability, carving his center cut. He stood there, in fear and trembling, half copout, half celebrant.

And this was not a cultural conclusion, out of the fifties and Kerouac, or out of the sixties and the hippies. I never got the impression that they, or the pop artists, or the rock stars, or the antiwar movement, or indeed his own troubles in his order, could be called his mainspring. He had a sensible, lucid, ironic, essentially modest view of himself and his talents. It kept him from parading around in his dust jackets and honorifics, like a jackal in a sable skin. It also kept him from whining or self-pity, even under great injustice. The style was the monk, neither victim nor victimizer.

Still, that center, that edge. He was an uneasy rider; he kept riding, uneasily. Is there any other way to keep going, to keep balance? He had the grace and skill and stamina to take the gospel seriously. And to take the consequences.

When he started writing poetry, he expended much time and trouble working through a problem that only later showed itself as a false problem. A famous essay posed the dilemma of the poet versus the contemplative. He lined up all the ambiguous areas, the rewards, fame, public notice, distraction, jostling images. And then compared these with the self-occlusion, darkness, of the monastic call. And came down pretty resoundingly on the side of austerity. Out damned spot!

He arrived shortly at a better sense of things, essentially a better sense of himself. False barriers dissolved. He started paying more attention simply to who he was, walking the earth with the rest of us, breathing the air, hearkening to a world that refused to let go of him. Now he had a third eye in his head, the monk's single vision. So his gifts did not hide out, atrophy in some root cellar.

The apocalyptic note is there in the poetry. By that I mean something more (so did he) than the terrified squeak of Chicken Little. Something more than powerlessness under the Bomb. It was an old notion: first, taking it all into account (this was a simple demand of truthfulness); then, the resolution, which in the final analysis was out of our hands, indeed, out of the hands of the bombers and bomb makers. But still, from another angle, the outcome was not out of our hands; it also depended, if we could trust the Bible, on the conviction, enterprise, courage of those who could speak up, stand somewhere.

He knew storm and calm, violation and promise, horror and resolution of horror. A human, a Christian. Long before most of us realized what impended, he faced the scientific apocalpyse in his "Original Child Bomb" (1962). It is a poem only in the most generous sense of the word, a kind of code rather, an incantation, a pastiche of quotes, with here and there a cunningly dovetailed, underplayed editorial. It concludes on a note of irony, prose flattened to earth, out of shape. First Truman's comment: "We found the bomb, and we used it." Then Merton:

> Since that summer, many other bombs have been "found." What is going to happen? At the time of writing, after a season of brisk speculation, men seem to be fatigued by the whole question.

The poem got around.

The poems are full of the penalties of awareness, especially in the matter of self-slaughter, war. One of the first of these was a touching threnody to his brother, John Paul. War snatched the life of that only brother, the first and last link to family. I had the impression Tom never stopped paying this cost. And some would say he never surpassed that early poem.

He told of an episode in his life, when he shagged John Paul away from games he and older kids were playing. John Paul went off crying, in the manner of a little boy desolate, rejected. My father once told me that on reading the story in *The Seven Storey Mountain*, he wept too, thinking of the later loss in World War II, and Tom's poem to his brother, which my father greatly admired.

I have the impression we will have to let the *Collected Poems* sink for a space to the bottom of the monk's pond, maybe for a few years. We are hardly equipped to judge the book rightly, for the present. Opinions are rampant about the author: He lived too long, he died too soon, he shouted too loud, he wrote too much, he didn't know where he was going, he was foolishly obedient, he should have kept quiet. As one mandarin Jesuit told me, Merton had no business messing around in that peace stuff. Ten years after death, the shock waves of grief and passion are still quite strong. Too much of what he warned of is dumping on us. We still cannot see him for what he was—what he was, I mean to his friends, which is my only interest. Those who knew him best and took him at his word and loved him as few are loved are still nearly tongue-tied.

How does one write when there are practically no standards for literacy, let alone excellence? When poetry, for instance, hovers around the culture like an all-night nurse a dying patient (temperature on the hour). Or like a priest around the dying (let's get that confession off our chest).

You do what Merton did, which is to say, you trust your own soul, knowing you are no more crazy and scarcely more sane than others. And you keep testing, sending poems out on the tide, and seeing what, if anything, comes back. Sometimes, mysterious inklings, sometimes nothing.

Strange how grandly disparate work, probings, experiments, finally, after years, stand out as reasonable, linked, sensible; the real accomplishment can be seen then for what it is.

The times are plain mad, a solid view. Therefore, writing has an element of nihilism, starting over, history not rearranged or finagled with, but a new start.

In primitive times (which are really our times, the clash of truth with empire), monks are nihilists in this sense. Merton ferreted them out, the founders of the new monasticism, and invited them in overnight so to speak: the freaks, the copouts, town criers, wandering fools, anarchists, *non serviam* placard holders. "Meet my friends," he said, with that foxy grin. He wanted to deinduct his order, an old and honorable task, to wean it from property and pride of place.

So his poetry has a kind of gritty irony. It was scandalous. He was getting simple, going to the roots. The poetry didn't seem

particularly religious, but what humanity shone through! And
it was a saving work, not only for the order, for the culture also.
The poetry is a bowel cleansing. He suffered a great deal from
colitis.

His friends, who hang around religious orders without quite
knowing what they're doing there, found him roughly in the
same fix. It was a sardonic ringaround; for the bosses didn't
know what they were doing either, only pretended they did,
waving the ferule, rapping knuckles, blessing make-work like
mad. Merton was a consolation of sorts, about as woeful and
tottery as ourselves. It was outrageous; he made a virtue out of
being uncertain (and yet quite certain), stuck in a cold cabin in
the woods (yet cherished and read and revered everywhere).
His faith was a kind of quirky swing of the pendulum; and he
made a virtue of faith, rare enough today.

His best poems, I think, came when he let those rhythms,
trapeze acts, move freely in mid air. If certainty goes hand in
hand with faith, he was a heretic indeed. And if one method
mastered was the ideal of poetic craft, he was a bad poet indeed.
But neither of these lofty ideals is verified today. And so he got
heard.

In the abstract, his situation was ideal. There he was in the
monastery, later in the woods, physically and intellectually on
his own. Nothing to do except slog on, the *itinerarium animae,* do
hard physical work so invigorating he took joy in it, be obedient
to tested principle and sapient superiors, say his prayers on the
hour. And more, enjoy considerable clout among the younger
monks, a house guru.

In other words. Life could have been a stifling disaster, a
world out of this world.

He couldn't bear it and began to improvise. From the day of
his first poems and the astounding public response to *The Seven
Storey Mountain.* What a large breadth Merton created for himself, pushing out and out; not for him the boxy space, *cubiculum
claustrum,* allowed the monk. Indeed, campus poets of today are
enormously more stifled, monkishly cloistered, ingrown, hide-

bound, than this prisoner of the Lord. Which might, by the way, account for the tooth of envy and its bite.

The Trappists hardly knew what they were letting themselves in for. How could they? Lo, the new convert, dipped and sheared, repentant of former lapses, eager of face, hot on the spoor of holiness. Trappists are specialists, midwives of the twice-born; but what were they to do with this twice-born adult? He was *pondus* and *gloria* both; he brought them renown; the young beat a path to the door, over which was lettered: *pax intrantibus.* The crazies came, too. What a burden!

He would have been easily disposed of had he become merely a nuisance of the garden variety, of which every order has its meed. But he grew to be a cosmic nuisance. He asked the questions that crowned heads never ask, in church or state: the nature of faith, the secular business of the world, other cultures and religions, music, poetry, photography; and war, war, war, the Bomb, the world becoming a grotesque ossuary. He kept probing; he wouldn't let go—how come, how come?

On the other hand, it was clear to anyone who could put on specs that he loved the monastery, its regimen, his fellow monks, the genius, energy, stillness. Much of the poetry is meticulously monastic, celebrational. He was at ease, eloquent, on just those themes that ought to be dear to monks. He wrote poems, lovely, tender poems, poems of an insider, about cemetery and seasons, the newly arrived and the dead, the harvesting, tree cutting, evensong, matins, ordinations, eucharist, silence. It was impeccable and ought to have been reassuring.

The trouble was the poems didn't stop there. They were like parasacraments, signs that led further. Or like the parables of Jesus, dynamite in the pumpkin patch. They were centers with electric fields around them. Anarchic experiments good and bad, secular interests, incendiary anger. And then the poems grew surreal; he worked on ideograms and strange typography, something called "concrete poems."

What was he after, what was he trying to do? He might say

(apart from things said above) he was trying to clear the rubble, he was trying to awaken people to the truth, he was trying to save what could be salvaged of lives and dignity, he was trying to show that atrophied human parts could indeed be turned on, a very spate of anger, indignation, joy, ecstasy even. That these were the proper functions of the soul awake. And judging by their neglect or virulent suppression by church and state, he was trying to say that most of us are half dead before we die. Half an eye on the world, half a dead ear bent to the sufferings of others, one-tenth of one pore open to the divine dew. And we call it Christianity. Christ!

One of the race of dedicated moles, this monk was spared so much! Causes of every stripe and cry, poetry readings in remote provinces, despairing calls by despairing humans to "come and save us," airport friskings, questions that get nowhere, answers that go nowhere, irregular hours, irregular prayer, irregular bm's.

Yet. Maybe he would have gained from a little exposure, some squirming under the big lights.

Out of the public glare as he was, he was not spared everything. His order was not subject to public opinion, was relatively untouched by change. This meant, among other things, a tough hand at the controls. Had the Trappists heard, in the late fifties and early sixties, of free speech? In less silent orders, this was also an issue.

In Merton's case, control was exercised to a degree that seems positively byzantine. The details, never publicly aired, were known to his friends. So was the cost, which included not only his personal grief and frustration, but the loss to us of an important public conscience.

The point is worth mentioning, since the repression and the call to a (spurious) obedience also drove him to write poetry. It was an exercise in sanity. An exorcism also.

He was hyperconscious of the social breakup, the church

breakup, whose tremors were underfoot day after day. He did something about this, indeed performed two services. He gave early storm warnings and a continuing diagnosis. Said, the human hand had slipped its glove. Into the glove crept a huge, mechanical claw: technocracy, statism, a bigger and bigger brother. The state Beast was now in command.

The Beast was also in the sanctuary; coercion of free speech and public debasement of the gospel, hand in glove. The Red and the Black, children of the same noisome *mater mundi*. This sense gets into the poetry. But he did not live to see the end of all this, which is upon us now.

When Merton was alive, it would have been a service to say "Whoa!" at times. He needed a Pound, to cut him to size. Short of that, we have in fact an enormous unpruned lifelong diary of everythings: trial and error and mood and conquest and pratfalls. And now and again, that mid-air triple somersault cannons into our hands. A poem!

·2·
THE ARTIST

One day in August of 1978, I read in *The Catholic Worker* a quite remarkable letter, addressed to Dorothy Day:

Dear Dorothy and Workers in the Vineyard:

Three times in my life I have been saved from fear. The first time, I was five years old. I ran into my parents' room crying, "What will I do if grandmother dies?" It was explained to me that there was no final parting; that my grandmother would then wait for me in heaven.

The second time, I must have been about ten or eleven. I read the story of the lepers of Molokai. I went into a kind of shock. It seemed to me prudent, to say the least, in a world where such fates were possible, to find a way of escape. All summer long, I haunted the swamps of Staten Island, dropping large stones into the ooze to test the door of life. The stones sank and disappeared, and gradually the obsession faded. One day, I took the book from its hiding place under the mattress and read it through. Somehow, Damien's heroism overshadowed the horror of life, and I was made to feel the Love that casts out fear.

The third time is now. I was given the verdict at Saint Vincent's Hospital. For two hours, I was in mortal terror. Then, a thought came to me. Not an experience, just a thought out

of Saint Teresa's wanderings along the roads of Spain. "The mules are packed, they are kicking, the road will be very rocky, but the destination is sure."
Saint Teresa encourages familiarity. This descendant of converts, very female, very stormy, very valiant, does not want us to fall back from the quest in awe of greatness. She asks that we join her in all our failing humanity, since there is nothing to disturb or afright us except, perhaps, vermin in uncomfortable inns.
Love to all from what Stanley Vishnewski used to call a Catholic Shirker.

I wrote the author, assuring her she would be welcome at the hospice for cancer patients where I was working part time. She was to come at her own pace. She wrote to thank me, and I began to visit her.

She lived with her husband in a two-room walkup in lower Manhattan; the apartment was the kind of sleazy relic that creates Dullsville even in Greenwich Village. You climb to a second floor, enter a court open to a patch of sky. The space is flooded with garbage bags. Apartment 2D is unlocked; she stands there leaning on her cane.
A frail Spanish woman, a classic face, vulnerable and strong-boned; somewhere between adamant and eggshell.

Born in the Argentine, she grew up on Staten Island. Her sculptures and paintings, which I had seen elsewhere, were superb. She said, "One day during the Vietnam war, they sent the FBI snooping around. One of them asked, 'How come your carvings are all in black? Are you pro-Negro [sic], making the saints black, and Christ?' I gave him a look. 'Now don't be silly. It's simple, the wood is black!' "

I brought flowers. Every week she exclaimed, as though it were the first, "How beautiful. I adore daisies (or roses or dahlias or snapdragons or carnations). How did you know?"

If a visit were impossible, we talked on the phone. She cradled the phone like a child, a lifeline. After two rings, I heard the plaintive childlike "Hello." And I thought, with relief, she's still alive.

In a corner opposite the bed and stove, stood the big, incongruous, rough-hewn workbench and the mallet. You looked at her and wondered: How did she ever raise that hammer against a hunk of ebony?

She said, "Every bone in my body is cracked. I want to go to St. Rose's, as you invited me. But not until the last moment. I can't leave my husband. We married late; for years and years he has been the best of comrades. But now my poor friend is confused and weak; he cries out for me in the night."
She called him "comrade" and "friend." I hadn't heard that before.

Through the doorway I saw a pair of legs stretched out on the cot in the room beyond. During the hour I stayed talking, the legs never once moved. It was only months later I saw his face.

"What happened to all the sculptures and paintings?"
"I sold them all to the same man. He promised they'd be kept together; he made a will to that effect."

She smoked a great deal. In the beginning it was, "Do you mind if I light up?" On a later visit, she lit one after another, smudged them out half-smoked. Her hands trembled terribly. "It's the pain. I'm in terrible pain." Was there anything to be done? "I don't know what, I've taken the biggest dose of drugs they'll allow me."

She reminisced like a recording angel.
"My father was an artist. One day, there was nothing to eat in the house. I was fourteen, already drawing and painting. My father said, 'I'm going out and see what I can sell in the street.' Mother said, 'Take some of Christina's drawings along.'

"And he came back grinning, with a pocket of money. It was my drawings he had sold!"

I brought her a recording and a book of my poems. She said grandly, "Now we will celebrate poetry week. Here are my translations of five Argentinians. You know, in the Argentine, a poet hasn't put in a good day unless he's delivered himself of a sonnet."

She pointed with her cigarette toward the next room where the silent comrade lay wrapt in his fog. "He used to write detective stories, and for years he did the chess puzzles for the *Times.*"

A long disquisition on the feminist movement. Her stern little face was puckered with concentration, the effort of clarity and exactness under the hammer of pain.
"Priests! Now they want to be priests! Let me tell you, I wouldn't go near a woman priest. They want admiration, oohs and ahs, they want to be like the men. I never needed to ape anyone, male or female, in the factory or art world or marriage. They could take it or leave it, me and my work."

She was sharp as a blue tack; her pronunciamentos left no doubts hanging in the air. She warned, "Remember now, I don't want you to go to jail anymore. That's all finished with. Promise."
I said only I would think about it.
(And when I was once more indicted after the Plowshares action, I prayed, up my sleeve so to speak, she would die before I went to prison. A prayer bitter as aloes; and the God of aloes answered it.)

One day: "I have a story for you about this jail business. It's a tale of Tolstoy, whom I adore. He tells of a pilgrim setting out on a long journey to some shrine or other. And in the course of his travels, he passes through a village where plague had struck. The sick and dying are all about, untended. So he stopped there and nursed and helped bury the dead. And one day it came to him: What had happened to his pilgrimage, his shrine and saint? Why, he was already there. This was his place of pilgrimage."

She pointed the cigarette at me like a ferule.

She would lie there, sounding off, a Cumaean sibyl: "The times grow worse, everything is breaking up. You have to stand somewhere. Otherwise you act like the maniacs during the Spanish war. They pulled down one of our glorious baroque churches, dust and ashes. There was a great crucifix in the chancel; they didn't quite dare destroy it; superstition held them back. But they scrawled a message on it in their delicate way. It went like this: 'He's ours at last.' You see? This is what the panic for change leaves us—a claim on Christ, and rubble."

Walking in, I asked invariably (what else was one to ask?), "How are you? What is the doctor saying?" One day she answered, "He's painting his rabbits."

"Painting his rabbits?"

"Yes. You remember, a renowned medico here in New York was involved in cancer research. He and his team were injecting rabbits with cancer cells and changing the color of the beasties. The theory was this would make it easier to detect cancer in humans. But one of the geniuses couldn't wait. So he painted his rabbits and made a big splash in the papers. Then they found him out and he was disgraced."

"But how is your doctor painting his rabbits?"

"Why, he says to me, 'You're in remission, you've been in remission for almost a year now. Next month it will be a year.' And all I see is a gleam in his eye. I'm his rabbit; he's going to break the Guinness cancer record or something. He's painting me."

She grew vehement, that little sack of bones.

"Painting rabbits! Does he think I'm a moron? Remission, remission the moon. All my bones cracking; the cancer's all through me."

Bad days and good. It was hard to tell the difference; she

made no great thing of pain. The chemotherapy was over and done with, by her choice. She wanted to be in charge of her own last days. Whose last days were they anyway?

I said to her one day on the phone, "You were in such pain yesterday, I could see it in your face. Why didn't you tell me?" And she, "Tell you, why should I tell you? The best pain killer I have is good conversation. You're my pain killer."

Her language was unquenchably old-fashioned.

"I wanted nothing of fame and fortune. And what I wanted most of all was given me." (There was a lucid vehemence in her eyes; it was that old Spanish spark, struck from rock.)

"I had good friends, interesting friends. There was this young Irishman just off the boats. He was wandering the streets, lonely as a stone in mid-air. One night he saw our sign: *Catholic Worker*. He raced in like the parched sailor he was.

"We'd walk the Lower East Side by the hour in the long, summer evenings. Now that he'd found a few kindred spirits, he was full of good humor, clicking his heels in the air.

"And just this year, he wrote me from somewhere in Westchester. Imagine, a grandfather, writing an old woman on her last legs."

"In those days I made a number of crucifixes. Some of them I took more care with than others; the most beautiful had mother-of-pearl lozenges embedded in the wood. A sea captain used to buy up whole batches and take them along on his next voyage, I suppose to sell them in southern ports. He got them from me for two dollars each. What he sold them for I never learned."

She must have been very beautiful in her young days.

I write that, then I think, what a foolish statement. How beautiful she is now! All that radiance, like the lifting light of morning; and fused, a mask, a permanence, the conquest of death before death. Who would not envy her, would not want to go like that!

No little puffs of valiance, like a lazy engine on a steep incline. No, her soul is steadied, poised, concentrated.

She becomes herself, day by day.

Month after month, I might have been dropping in on someone slightly ill, on the mend. Hers was a deliberate, finespun tactic, a fiction of the soul. To despise the Big Bad Wolf, reduce him to No Big Deal. He didn't own her before he owned her. And even when the big payment came due, would he have prevailed? She thought not. Those disdainful, worldly eyes; you could read their large braille: By no means!

She had a slight Latin cadence, her *d*'s and *t*'s were velvet. She said, "You can see from the way I talk I'm not adjusted to this world."

Said, "Picasso and some of the others make me the enemy of modern art. Or at least the enemy of their art. They begin with the noblest intention: Let me show you how horrible life is today. And they end by showing you something else: how to become part of the horror."

She pointed to the far wall, her painting of Saint Francis and the wolf. "The model was already dead when I painted Francis. He was a Russian emigré who spent his last years trying to keep his wife from going mad. He didn't realize she was already flamboyantly mad. They had a retarded son. I used to trudge up to Rockland State Hospital every week to see the boy; he died there.

"You see why I couldn't be very active around the Catholic Worker? There were always these poor souls who needed me, one to one. It was discouraging, but what could I do?"

One day: "Do you think it would be all right if I didn't go to the hospital right away?"

"I think anything you want to do will be all right."

She settled back to savor this cold comfort. What she wanted I could read in her eyes: to stay with her "comrade" as long as she could eke out her life.

And one day when I came in, I saw through the kitchen doorway, in the little box of a bedroom, a disembodied form, a long gray beard, two eyes regarding me. The apparition said not a word, kept staring in my direction. Here at last was the "comrade," and I was evidently a cause of wonderment to him, as he to me.

I gave her a small crucifix I had brought from France for my mother. She palmed it in silence, nearly broke down. "It is very beautiful, better than anything I could have made."

Said: "This war of the sexes! Let me say this: From eight years on, since I discovered I was a talent [she did not say, "I was talented" or "I had talent"]—since then, I have been helped by men; they have been my brothers."
And I: "But you told me once your father favored your brother over you."
"True; and that boy was by no means brilliant."
She shrugged, lifted her hand, paused. "It was that way in the family; the son was everything. In spite of that, I survived, to do my work, have my friends, set my own pace."
"But you were strong; and many are talented and are not strong. And so they are ruined."
She leaned forward. Her cat's gleam told me I had lost another round. "This you do not understand. To be strong is to be talented, to be talented is to have strength. These are by no means two things; they are one thing and the same."

One day the comrade met me at the door as I came in; on his feet at last. A brawny, infinitely sad-eyed old man, he shook hands with me as though I were a ghost. Then he turned about, mortified, lost. She said gently, "Now you can go, dear, read, take your rest." And he shuffled off.

One day, the pain consuming, beyond bearing, she cried out, "It is you who are keeping me in this world!"

She passed her Sundays like the Creator, at rest.
She earned that rest; she beat her way through the days,

creating a path in a jungle, somewhere at the edge of the world. Sundays her presence and converse were grandly sabbatarian.

One day: "From now on, I call you 'Daniel.' " (This though she had been punctilious and regal about "Father.") She lay there, savoring my wonder.

"In poetry, you are great or you are nothing. We do not call Gerard Manley Hopkins 'Father Hopkins,' do we?"

She smiled, sat back, palmed another cigarette.

Another day she pressed a few notes into my hand. "These I wrote when I could not sleep."

> There is a sect of Hassidic Jews who recently lost their rabbi. This rabbi taught that to kill is forbidden; he taught that a man who has spilled blood cannot claim to be a Jew.
> Something of the courage and faith of this man must be shown by Christians. Like the poor benighted Spanish workers, we must reclaim Christ because "He is ours"; but unlike them, we will not destroy his church.

With the help of friends, we came to an arrangement whereby she could receive her drugs and be helped with housekeeping. The news all but drained the agony from her face. Now she would not be carted off to a hospital, leaving her eighty-six-year-old comrade to perverse winds of fortune.

We talked about poetry. It was not uplift she saw in my work, nor morally impeccable sentiments. It was life, and she said so. Added: "The poems will be at my side, along with your mother's crucifix, all the days of my life."

"Here are some notes," she would say. "They are my way of coping with the pain that visits me during the night."

> I began drawing as a little girl in the kitchen at home. The servants brought the drawings to my mother. When we came to America, I won the Wanamaker citywide contest for schoolchildren. I was eight and a half. My mother began to take a serious interest in my work.
> When I was fourteen I started to work at the Metropolitan

Museum, drawing from sculpture. After that, I went to the
National Academy of Design. This was the depth of the
depression; the family finances collapsed. I went on the Art
Project as an art teacher. My work was noticed and sent
around on exhibit.

At a friend's studio, I tried my hand at wood carving and was
successful at first try. It was a child, life-size, a rather large
piece. At an exhibit it was called "excellent" by a critic of the
World Telegram. I did a series of children from then on. One
was in marble, all were sold.

Then I discovered the Catholic Worker.

My family were not practicing Catholics. My father was
brought up by monks, my mother by the Madames of the
Sacred Heart. My father tried a synthesis of Darwin and Catholicism; apparently the conflict between science and the
church disturbed him. My mother continued as a Catholic—in
everything but practice. She knew nothing else.

I fell into the Catholic Worker without any trouble. I decided
to do traditional (not conventional!) religious art. The image
of the Virgin Mother at the Worker is from this period.

I made crosses, many of them, angels, a very good St. Theresa
in fruitwood, a small virgin with a silver crown. The crosses
started out very unconventional, black Christs, worker
Christs; but I returned to the more conventional image, which
I found could not be improved on. Before I got sick I had
thought of trying my hand at a rather large Christ in dark
wood. I only think about that now.

The Spanish civil war broke out. This was a very emotional
period for any Spaniard. The attitude of Spaniards toward the
church was (as usual) split along class lines. The Orders that
had been busy manufacturing young gentlemen (I am afraid
this includes yours) were persecuted. Those that taught the
poor and all nursing sisters were protected by the militia.

I caught the war fever and stopped going to the Worker, and
even became somewhat estranged from Dorothy, who was
really neutral, a pacifist.

From this period date my black slave women. They were not
actually meant to be slaves, but images of oppression. These

were bought up. The ones you saw were only part of a collection, bought by a radical labor lawyer. The money that my doctors have been eating up came mostly from him. Toward the end of this period, I made that head. You asked, "Was it the head of a saint?" It was not the head of a particular saint, but an image of saintliness. I had seen at the museum some Indian heads that were without characterization, but imbued with an otherworldly spirit. I tried to do the same with the Christian spirit.

At this time, my father died and my mother came to live with me. I had to take a job. After a few adventures at a jewelry factory, at the bench and as designer, I became a medical secretary.

During these years, I painted, after the day's work. Some of my paintings of children and of flowers were good. I sold them to dealers through a gallery in the Village. When my mother became too frail, I stopped working and lived on savings.

My mother died; and then in rapid succession I lost most of my friends. At this time, I married Arthur.

Then I went to work in earnest. I painted Saint Francis and the Wolf; also the mother and child. All were meant to be religious, though none were on religious subjects. They were, like the head of the saint, meant to convey a religious feeling. I also made angels, not conventional ones, but creatures with wings. I carved a very strange horse's head with a human face, a horse out of Swift, the horse nobler than man. This piece has been liked by everyone. The face is the same as Saint Francis; it is fallen back and bears a look of triumphant suffering. It represents the animal and the divine in man. It has even been liked by people who just like horses.

Although I had at different times different intentions about my work, I realize now that all of it is similar in spirit. Dorothy and others have shown surprise at the peace my works express. A young black man said he thought my work was good "because of its serenity" (which he pronounced "seeereeeni-ty"). I think it is because, being a woman, intellectual doubts about the justice of God, which of course I have had, never touched the heart of my work.

The production sounds very big in the telling, but is in fact rather small, though large enough to surprise me now. I am not sorry that a lot of it is scattered. I never used to sign my early pieces, because of romantic admiration for the carvers of medieval cathedrals. It does not really matter to me to leave a name. I think some of these pieces (if the world lasts) will survive because some people have loved them.

And the Catholic Worker has my Virgin Mother. I consider that a great honor for my work.

One day she presented me with her *Saint Francis and the Wolf.* It was the last painting in her possession.

Her quirky, formal, delicious tongue was equal to the occasion. "The head of Saint Francis is the head of a friend of mine, long dead, a Russian. I say to you what he said of Dostoievski: 'A long pitchfork sticks out of the hay mow and tries to call itself a needle.' "

We were able to get competent medical help; her life lengthened out. Then I was offered a teaching stint on the West Coast and had to so inform her. She was desolate for a while, but came back strong. "Daniel, I think I'm going to last until you return. Of course it's right for you to go; they need teachers like you. And now I'm in good hands, thanks to you."

Her mind grew lax, like a warm clutch of blind kittens when a hand reaches in among them. Whose hand, which kitten?

She watched her art disappear as her life waned. "All things for use, one only for desire." Her glance on the world of objects, faces, flowers, horses, gods, was the look of an artist who had once staked a claim. But now was the time of letting go.

What would seem opinionated or narrow in others, in her was a simple cast of the line. She was superbly certain of a catch. It was no mere piscatory skill; she was goddess of both sea and land, working the rod, working the hook.

No wonder I was taken.

As for the world—ideas, chaos, breakup, women's lib, men in

the saddle, wars and rumors of wars—she sat like a blind sibyl
in the black mouth of a cave. Death had moved against her; it
was a declaration of war. This was the point at which passion
was not only legitimate, it was a last-ditch cry in favor of existence. There she sat, day after day, month after month, in the
mouth of the squalid cave. The mouth that, at any moment,
might choose to snap shut; at any moment, possessive and en-
gorging as it was, might choose to make an end of her.

Our ritual developed, so precise it might have been the score
of a ballet.

Ring the buzzer, open the door, twenty steps down the Tom-
Thumb corridor, up the blind stair, cross the court. Her door
is ajar. "Come in, Daniel." There are flowers to be unwrapped
and admired and put in place. Her walker must be shifted to one
side. She arranges herself on the bed, a minimal shift of position
will be required of her poor bones for an hour or so.

I move the table to one side and pull up a chair (the only
chair). It is like tea time Behind the Looking Glass. The preci-
sion of each move, the inching of furniture to left or right,
banishment of impediments to speech and sight—there is
economy here, of time and place. The grave is narrow, the time
short. Now listen to me, speak to me.

In a dark mood, she wrote this:

> I have tried not to mind embarrassment
> since the day I discovered
> that we are more upset by our blunders
> than by our mean actions
> I am not outside the malaise
> My happiness consists in having conquered the malaise
> while living in the center of it
> The malaise is the fear
> that *human* may be after all
> only a blighted species
> unfit as any animal
> a sport in the house of nature
> and fated to bring all down in ruin

Against this
I call up the faces of my loved ones
and refuse to give them up to death.
It is because I have won in this fight
that I am happy.

From California I sent her a picture card "instead of flowers."
It was a Picasso image, a child and a dove.

The painting is not better than flowers, but it is just as good.
At his best, Picasso was a tender, even feminine artist; as if his
was the work of a female genius. This must have troubled him.
Good Spanish Muslim that he was, he never abandoned a
woman and never rejected a child.

Even the way in which he lost himself is to his credit.

In 1914–1918 he was very far from home, from Andalusian
doves and children and sentimental folk songs. The enthusiasm for new forms in art he correctly saw as decadence
and disaster. As people close to him went mad or committed
suicide, he wrote that this was caused by undue interest in the
unconscious and by admiration for insanity.

Picasso thought he would be another Goya and report the
disaster; but a Goya he was not. In some ways Picasso was the
better artist; but Goya was a stalwart and valiant soul.

There may have been better artists than Picasso, but none I
liked more. In old age he returned to his simple youth and
made lovely portraits of young girls and children. These he
did not sell, but kept for himself.

He could not bear to part from his past. Money went to his
women and children, to the houses that were to hold his best
work, and to the Spanish refugees. When he visited them in
the south of France, whole towns turned out to welcome their
prince. These were radicals, veterans of the fight against fascism. They would not have forgiven him his wealth unless he
had shared it.

Now I have talked you to death; but I only meant to thank you.

You could never forget she was Spanish; it was there, in the slight lilt, the gentle roll of vowels, the ever-so-slightly-lisped consonants. But most of all in her cast of mind, which was impetuous and outrageous and delightful beyond telling.

I returned from California; indeed she had made it. But she was thinner, more wraithlike than ever; as if she were being whittled away, a bare bone, a whistle for whittler death.

She was still opinionated to the nostrils. No doubt death was nearing, lurking closer. But she yielded not an inch of her mind.

I confessed how strange I had found Berkeley, its mix of hubris and *dolce vita*. How utterly estranged I had been from the seminary scene.

She pushed further, as usual. "The trouble is there shouldn't be any such thing as theologians. That's no way to spend a life. And they've done great harm, mauling the gospel, letting the powerful get away with more and more."

We inched our way toward the nuclear question, the same dread sitting heavy on both of us.

"Don't forget, Daniel, we've seen all this before. People have eaten people, murdered one another, all for the noblest reasons. In Mexico, when they began examining the Toltec images, they found inches of dried human blood caking the statues. In any case, we have no assurance the world is to go on and on.

"I'm going home soon, you see. Earlier than you or others. But everyone is going home. And who's to say it's not to happen in one great blast?"

But where does Christ come in?

"He doesn't come in. He's already in. He gave us no more assurance on such matters than we might gain from a reading of our own history. But we've been consistently blind for as long as we were (purportedly) gifted with seeing. Every war shows it; we've always wanted the kind of weapons we can now brandish in the world."

Listen. when I was six
my father brought indoors
a wounded blue heron.
He set the bird gently
in a box by the stove.
We did everything possible to save its life
but the beautiful bird died.
I learned from that, as well as from much reading
if a species is greviously wounded or diseased
you accomplish nothing
though you try by every means to save it.
I ask myself—
is humankind so afflicted, so diseased
that no efforts will avail?
I think nothing will avail.

"You know, one of those theologians once asked me, 'Tina, do you believe in eternal life?'

"I said to him, 'Shake me up in the middle of the night, and I'll undoubtedly say I do. But don't ask me to bend my waking reason to such a question.' "

(She leaned forward.) "Do you know what their trouble is? They think they can reason their way to God. They remind me of someone trying to drink coffee through his ear."

From time to time she would announce clues as to my identity. And I, who invariably wince at so bootless an exercise, found it, coming from her, intriguing in the extreme.

Said: "I've been thinking of who you are. First off, you're not a saint; that's too soon.

"Nor a hero; that's too easy.

"What you are is this: You're a messenger. And I don't want to die until I hear all the message."

There came a time when she was in truth dying. The signs were there: short breath, dry mouth, glazed eyes, fever, great pain. Our agreement stood; it was time to move on. We summoned an ambulance; in the stuffy little kitchen-bedroom, we were at great trouble to lift her onto a stretcher; her bones like flimsy shells strung one to another, she could be broken by a single maladroit move.

We got her, nip and tuck, alive across lower Manhattan, every pothole evoking groans to wring the heart. We backed to the rear door of St. Rose and wheeled her in, strapped to the cot like a papoose, a body with hardly more breath than a tucked blanket. And in the doorway stood a sister, the invariable wan and compassionate smile, to stroke her face and welcome her to St. Rose. It was the ancient, unfailing magic, a courtesy of soul that keeps death at bay.

Outside the window, a park lifted its autumn trees; it was a sight her long illness had denied her, in that hideous, stifling room on Macdougal Street.

"The trees are so beautiful," she whispered.

They were by no means remarkable trees, only dun sycamores that pass in autumn from uninspiring gray-green to less inspiring gray-brown. It struck me with a pang: How long it has been since she has seen a tree of any hue or form at all!

When the very ill are conscious, they seem less ill, as though a mysterious hand kept thumping them awake. But when they fall into sleep or coma, what a change takes over! Slack jaw, pallor, remoteness, feverish dew of hand and brow.

I came into the ward carrying a bouquet of carnations. Walked within range, stood there. She focused, knew me, the withered arms went up, a Spanish gesture, grand and baroque. For the flowers, for me, what a welcome—and all wordless.

Over the vapid boom! boom! of the television, I leaned close to catch that otherworldly wisp of voice, like the smoke of a quenched wick.

"I must tell you," she whispered, "I had an extraordinary vision yesterday. Everything reconciled: my life, my family. Backward and forward, this world, other world, everyone dancing. And someone making amends, reconciling, doubling gain for all loss. There my nephew dances, and you, and my mother and father, and Dorothy, everyone."

All the while she was tenderly touching and stroking and lingering over my face as I bent to her; a touch lighter and more exacting than any I have known. As though in her blind journey she were memorizing the outline of a life she must say farewell to.

"You are there, Daniel, and those I love, and we shall be there together. I have no fear. I go with all my heart."

· 3 ·

THE AUNT

In 1906 Brigid Berrigan entered the Sisters of Charity in New York, following what was becoming a family pattern. Her uncle had entered the seminary in Albany, New York, in 1864, after years of indentured slavery on the land, a plowboy. Since she was sixteen, Brigid had been a teacher in an upstate New York country school, as will be described in greater detail later in this chapter. Her father died when most of his children were still in swaddling bands, so her vocation was long delayed; one did not lightly enter the convent when there were hungry mouths at home.

Her order shortly put uncommon responsibilities on her. She was endlessly "missioned" to one school or another, teacher or principal or both, usually local superior of the community as well.

We younger fry of the clan soon got used to the immutable fact: Sister Josephine (her new name in the order) was someone to be reckoned with, one who, in the tradition of final judgment, demanded and received a periodic accounting.

The accounting was rendered during her summer visits "to home." Indeed, her arrival was a matter of long discussion and some apprehension for weeks before the event. Quasi-military headquarters would be set up on Matson Avenue, the family longhouse where three other aunts, in rectitude unrelieved, held court. There, arrangements were monastic, monogamous, clan-ridden, the participants tough as nails and durable as only transplanted Irish can be.

On her home visits, Sister Josephine, like the duchess in the poem, was not to be conjured more than a hundred feet distant from her carriage; in this case, our consumptive Model T Ford. She carried about her an atmosphere of incalculable mystery; it hovered about her reticule, her long-coned outer hat, very like a witch's, wreathed in black tulle and worn over an inner bonnet, the two attached under the chin in spectacular bows. Skirts to her dainty heels, a small or long cape, tiny shoes completed the sacred costume.

She survived waves of New York immigrants, displaced persons, generations of children, half-mad and wholly marvelous nuns "in her charge." In her generation, the slavery of women —housekeeping, tilling fields, bearing children—was hardly relieved when a woman entered the convent. Brigid Berrigan, reincarnated as Sister Maria Josephine, remained a slave, albeit a consecrated one: In classroom and laundry and scullery and chapel. And yet in our family, among the children, indentured to parochial school and its principalities and powers, she seemed a figure of glamor and repose.

I carry her face through a lifetime, through all states and permutations. Her face of youth looks out from the old photos, an ivory Irish beauty, perky, half-amused, of deep-browed thoughtfulness. What the Quakers name an inner light was hers; at thirty-four it claimed her quite, led her deeper and deeper into that conflict and repose and totally unglamorous service called religious life. She was the most beautiful and talented of a generation whom immigrant parents bore into a world of bleak and land-locked poverty. But what she made of it all!

She had a mind to match her face and wit to spare; her extraordinary cat's eyes took the world's measure early on, claimed it for her ransom. When those eyes rested on me and my brothers, we quailed under judgment—malfeasance, bickering, laziness, and above all that abuse of the mind that her glance cut into like a whip. And even while we fumed and muttered excuses, we knew we were beneficiaries of a rare form of love. Someone was demanding that our disused, somnolent souls come alive, that we begin, in her inelegant, characteristic phrase, "to make something of ourselves." (She was, like many of her generation, much given to the boot-strap Pelagian view: You made it in the world, your passage lubricated with sweat and tears, and God tagged along, clocking the miles for merit.)

And I know we loved her too, with that complicated mix of awe, ignorance, and distancing, which we also name love of God.

(I intersperse my memories with those of a nun who lived in her community for some years and wrote a series of memoirs of my aunt some years before her death.)

You've asked for this. [The "you" evidently refers to the community archivist.] So you're getting it. . . . I was all excited when I heard you wanted some memories of Sister Josephine. . . . But then when I began to think, and think and think, I wished I could do a laundry instead. That at least would be limited and specific. This task is immense. To tell about *her isn't hard, but to reproduce the whole personality—that is no joke. . . . I can't do anything but leave you the big part of the job—and simply ramble on. . . .*

Everything had to be in prime shape for sister's arrival on summer holiday. The farm, dour and poor enough at best, must show a good face: yard raked, barn immaculate. My mother stood properly at the door in welcome. The best dishes were out, the silver gleaming. This was a visit of state, and as such, occasioned one of the few banquets of those lean years, matched only by Christmas and Thanksgiving.

By later, more affluent standards, the menu was plain enough; and it was also invariable over the years, a meal my mother could turn out with reasonable style and assurance. Meatloaf, scalloped potatoes, a salad, apple pie, coffee.

But first there was a tour of the fields and barns. The sisters paced along with my father, he on his Sunday behavior, strained joviality leaking from his seams. The sisters, Josephine and her "companion," either Sister Madeleine (whom we adored) or

Sister Margaret (equally abhorred). Like two shadows of shadows in the brilliant noon, they plunged into the ankle-high corn, our small dog tearing ahead, chasing improbable rats.

Thence, eventually into the cool of the barn, rendered unprecedentedly antiseptic by application of brush and lime, clean straw under the beasts, their mildly astonished faces turned toward us as the procession entered.

And Josephine, her fine, patrician nose on high, sniffing the air: "Oh, that good, clean, ammonia smell!"

Our eyes met, Phil's and mine. Ammonia? We thought of the phenomenon, referred to it vulgarly and frequently, as plain old cow piss.

When sister was our superior, she had passed into her seventies. She had gone through all those phases of life in which people show excess of enthusiasm or fastidiousness about other people's opinions, an exaggerated excitement. When asked a question, she'd say, "I presume so," looking beyond somewhere. Or, "No, sister," simply. She was old, in other words. Her face was wrinkled, in a very interesting way. The fine lines around her eyes did two things: They did not make her weary, or stern, or calculating. They rendered the large eyes deep and wide apart and interested, curious and kindly. . . . She traveled through time and space more easily than anyone I ever knew.

At age eighteen, I announced I was entering the Jesuits. The news generated considerable excitement in the family, mine being the first such venture of our generation. At the Annual Visit, I was accosted in private by Josephine. I knew she had no large enthusiasm for the Jesuits; still, on the salvation market, they were beyond doubt a gold-edged investment. Her delight was evident; it showed in her eyes, the childlike gaze of excitement she turned on me.

But she restrained herself. She had always inclined in her dealings with youth a little to the side of David Copperfield's aunt. Boys were not constitutionally virtuous; when they appeared so, probably some trick lay up their sleeve.

So her joy on this occasion verged on the minatory. "Daniel," she said with severity, "don't forget, a Berrigan doesn't show the white flag!"

I had received my marching orders. If I failed, I was to be allowed to return, like a warrior from Thermopylae, only on my shield.

You asked about her human failings. Right here is where her accusers would pause. Accusations would have to go on in low tones, for shame, in the presence of that wide-eyed sincerity. Hers was not so remote and abstruse a train of thought as you might think, either. Sister would be seized by preoccupations and convictions that filtered through other levels, all levels where the Big Bully was exploiting the self-respecting and re-served. To sit quietly, follow her, was a calm and refreshing journey.

Here comes another snare in trying to portray her. You think she is impractical, vague and all loose ends. But a hundred times a day she would prove just the opposite.

For instance, you felt the cold steel of her inquiry if you made a slip on the office card file. She herself registered every student's every mark. She spent Columbus Day, Lincoln's Birthday, Decoration Day, long holidays doing it. That is typical of her; her contribution to any cause is (I suspect on principle) always hidden and slow and permanent—and colossal. . . . I say this is probably so, on principle, because she told me her sisters and brothers used to call blowhards "small potatoes." Their father was a hard-working Iowa farmer and the great idol of her childhood. She heard him tell how he scorned farmers who sold barrels of potatoes, big solid ones on the top, and the bottom filled with the small, soggy ones.

Josephine was the only one of my father's family who did not disdain my mother. Cast among the Irish, my mother dwelt close to disaster, her emotional strength tried in ways both subtle and hectoring.

But that is another story. The point here is that two extraordinarily gifted and gritty women looked one another in the eye over a period of years, took each other's measure, and turned away, satisfied with what they saw.

A point of contention: My mother, as far as I could judge, never bought the "higher-vocation" theory, as applying to clergy. Indeed, her response to "the cloth" was no matter of heavy breathing before a purportedly sacred status; her glance, upon whatever faunum resting, was remarkably untrammeled. I well remember in this regard her response when I first told of my purpose of becoming a priest. She said laconically (though I could sense elation and pride as well), "If you're going to act like some of the current crop, don't waste your time." It was, in the medical department, a salutary deflation.

In Josephine, my mother saw something she characterized as the "genuine article." I think their love of the poor, their standing at the side of those who had few to speak for them, drew the two together. There was no humbug between them, no religious cant, which was all the more remarkable, as humbug was a large item among Irish Catholics, and the clergy stood, in Berrigan eyes, above discussion, let alone criticism.

Her white hair used to stream from under her cap sometimes, and she had many old clothes for laundering and holiday mending. She loved hand-me-downs. She loved poverty with a passion. Her mouth, even in repose a straight line, betrayed a spirit that was unconquerable. Once when a superior apologized while handing her a bitter task, she laughed, "You know I love the smoke of battle!" She didn't though. She was finely molded and sensitive, but what she loved was sporting blood.

It was 1947, I had long since folded away any white flag, or lost it, or perhaps burned it once and for all. In any case, my stock was high with Josephine; I was mainline Berrigan by now—a teacher, a card-carrying Jesuit.

She was then in her late seventies, had suffered a stroke, was genteelly referred to as "retired" to the old Foundling Hospital on Lexington Avenue in the East Seventies. It was a dingy, haphazard, high-ceilinged place, slapped together wing by wing, an architecture out of Bosch. One passed through arcades and courts and upper enclosed bridges to reach the foundlings in their cribs, abandoned children, orphans and love babies.

I came in each month from Jersey City to visit my aunt in New York. The visits were both pro forma and blood linear; they had a charming character, both juridical and warm of heart.

A sister would ensconce me in the front parlor, the inevitable founding fathers and mothers regarding me somberly from their gilt frames. A shuffling step in the corridor, a slow opening of the eight-foot oak door, and a little, shrunken woman appeared, leaning on the arm of a younger sister.

It was her eyes that riveted one; those, and the heart-breaking smile.

She settled gingerly in the nearest straight chair, her right leg (the "bum one") straight out before her. You noted that, though her shoes were as worn as parchment and inevitably second-hand, they were thinnest at the front tip of the uppers, a spot that could wear through only from constant kneeling.

Taking stock of age and illness, she had organized her life anew. No more big projects indeed. But did that mean no projects at all? She bridled at the thought: "One might as well be under six feet."

She looked around her in the great, inefficient barracks where so many lives had their inauspicious start: unwanted children, infants abandoned in doorways, under trestles, in ash cans; there, beyond all doubt, she had been sent to die.

She was not, however, dying; not for a while. She was merely growing older; a different matter indeed. In view of that, of time at her disposal, what was to be done?

One wing of the hospital was given over to the care and shelter of single mothers. They had come to bear their infants and, in most cases, to sign them over for adoption. Fortified with her cane, my aunt wandered among these land-locked folk, got acquainted.

Shortly she learned how rudimentary were their skills of writing and reading; Spanish or black or poor white, their common predicament nothing as simple as unfortunate pregnancy. What indeed was to become of these women in the great city, poor and semiliterate as they were?

Here was a task indeed. Josephine assembled books, Spanish readers, vocabularies, spelling exercises. She began to work with her new charges one-to-one.

Wasn't this exciting? Her face would glow. She was useful once more; she was back in her element.

Self-possessed and huffy as ever, she told how a visitor ("Irish, and a man, wouldn't you know") marveled in hushed tones at how fortunate she was to have entered "so holy a vocation, to have missed the sin and squalor of the world."

It was the old mortician argument in which Irish piety excelled: better dead, and safe at last, than on your feet in the messy, folly-ridden world.

She scoffed: "I could have told him a thing or two about sin and squalor." And beyond doubt she could have.

She had a beautiful face. Her nose was chiseled from marble, and her expression was a mixture of curiosity and laughter, or a smile coming on—when she was not angry.

She was so small and dainty of stature that we enjoyed the picture we imagined of her young days. In "upstate New York" in a country school, the big boys were so tough and hard-skinned that when the local authorities used to try a man out for teacher (one teacher for all grades), they would fire a shot from a pistol at the wall, just above the candidate's head. If he winced, he lost the appointment.

But when she applied for the job and the officials saw her, they did not put her through the ordeal. She taught boys who were literally twice her size, and the public school system there has never forgotten her. The men she turned out were, in two instances, the authors of texts we younger sisters used in St. Peter's High School. Others became engineers, professionals, plain folk of wisdom.

Why do I remember her with such sharp vividness? Her picture is on my wall, an enlarged snapshot from some primitive box camera, taken in days when a photo of a nun was as rare as hens' teeth.

Old age, far from quenching, could but quicken her. Her time was short; but then, was not all time short? *Todo le pasa.* She took the mystics at their word and went on.

"What was I reading?" she would ask. The question was a mere prelude to an announcement: what *she* was reading, and the discussions her current book gave rise to among the sisters.

The clan had been a long time recovering from the wounds of Al Smith's defeat at the hands of religious bigots in 1928. At that time the luck of the Irish had run out, all but drowned in a tide of nativism. "Oh, they showed what they thought of us!" she would exclaim. But her voice held no bitterness.

We would shuffle through the draughty old corridors of the hospital, hand-in-hand, she talking avidly of her "children," the infants, the mothers. Discreet black, the clerical greenhorn, the nun who had endured it all and was so near vanquishing. Lately, she told me with delicious malice, the community was resisting the blandishments of Cardinal Spellman, his eye on the place, his chancery hacks coming and going, determined to "run the place more efficiently" (she would intone it with a twist of the lip that said all).

Then her mind would rove back in time, to the ebb and high tide of immigrants, the dispossessed, the street people. Even in memory, she moved among the victims, at whose side she had begun, from whom with stubborn, innate sense of rightness she refused to budge.

Her lists of the poor were ample as a borough telephone directory. . . . Many of them took advantage of her generosity; she knew that. "If they are willing to get a few cents by that method, they're pretty down and out," she'd say, opening her tin change box. She herself would go to the parlor or the back door to see what could be done to salvage some hope.

A very old man whom the sisters and everyone called "Pop" came quite regularly, with shameless, hair-raising distortions of the truth. The truth was we used to see Pop stretched out very red-faced and fast asleep in the afternoon sunshine on some public bench. He had stories about how hard he worked and how poor he was. The convent cereal dishes, halves of loaves of bread, and Sister Josephine's jams, and hot coffee—all these were put before Pop after hours. Sister would then let him sweep the cellar to prove his self-respect.

Trousers, overshoes, shoes, gloves—these came out of the clothes pile for Pop. He used to hold sister with long stories of his odyssey, and she would lay out the law philosophically; then she'd come up the path chuckling.

She could be firm, too. I have seen her like a thunder cloud on a Sunday morning on the threshold of a poor shack in a neighborhood alley— calling, "Master McHugh, get up out of that bed!" And the storm continued, silent and ominous, until young McHugh's feet were on the floor. She flung back over her shoulder, "I'll be waiting down at the church. There is no time to dawdle, young man."

She lived into her nineties—frail, all eyes, clairvoyance, and will. She visited the family less often. Her generation almost gone, she was a ghost among the living.

I do not recall any complaints.

As she lived on, a field of fioretti grew up around her. One sister told me that, years before, my aunt had summoned the young sisters from their morning prayer, led them to the house of a poor family whose mother lay ill. They cleaned, prepared breakfast, got the children off to school. "This is your prayer," was all she said to the sisters.

"None of us ever forgot that," sister added.

I could count at least seventy so-called hopeless students she lifted up and urged onward. Her classroom (she taught on and off from nine to five every day but Sunday) sometimes swarmed with young people of all ages after three o'clock. They had not done their work for the day. In one corner, a high school senior memorized chemistry valences. Up at the board, two fifth-graders stumbled and scowled through long division; a group of first-year Latin students would be learning the day's vocabulary; by her knee a baby would be poring over his primer. They used to go home with a conviction that unattainable things were actually within their power, a burning of their cheeks, enthusiasm starting up in them, to study and make the grade.

I often wonder, loving her as I do, holding her before me far more vividly than I do many of my contemporaries—I wonder what she would have made of our times, of the directions we opened (sometimes with a sense of scouting new territory, more often like blind gophers, underground). I think of her sister's daughter, who wrote us a furious letter, renouncing the whole tribe for the sins of Phil and myself. And (cousin went on) "for the misbegotten shame of having her son name his son Philip Daniel. The shame of it."

Would Josephine have approved our way, would she have looked on our world as we do? I can merely speculate, even as

I honor the moral coherence of a life that grasped a vision and held firmly to it through storms, burdens, sea changes, losses, betrayals, through that final redoubt of old age, where even genius must give over. I think her life brought her to the threshold of our own. More, that she pushed us through a narrow door guarded fearfully by death the dog.

She abominated outline books, all short-cut methods. She considered them traitorous to the children.

She believed in essay-type questions. She maintained that these taught the student to build up thought and express it wholly.

She had nothing but steel and thunder clouds for the teacher who complained of too many papers to correct. For her chemistry or Latin or English students, she was continually hectographing and correcting papers.

She highly approved rigid training of the memory. She said she'd like to experiment with a civics class by teaching the Constitution thoroughly, making them learn it by heart and explain it, and keep to that alone.

She taught history and civics not only from texts, but from her father's viewpoint, his attitude toward Lincoln, the rise of the railroads and steel industry during her childhood. She was not dogmatic. Her technique was to throw out a question that had always puzzled her when she was growing up and let the class come back with whatever they could.

How did she see that mysterious, old-fashioned "religious vocation"? Around this point, she turned on a pivot that was diamond-hard. Obedience, poverty, chastity, and above and beyond and within all, a reality Gandhi would celebrate—service.

Her world, the world she grew up in, could hardly have been called well ordered or just. It was a world of rock-bottom poverty, illness, early death. For the women, mother church laid it down hard; they bore large families, or they were "gifted with" the only other choice, a "religious vocation."

Her sisters went their own way. Three remained unmarried; one was a highly skilled secretary to a congressman, one a trained nurse, a third a schoolteacher. They had hearkened to the advice of their Uncle Will, who urged them from seminary to move off the farm, where "there was no future." And to "help one another gain an education that would fit them for the world." It was sound advice, and the family eventually flourished.

Her youth was dramatically beautiful and vivid in her memory. She recalled lying atop the hay wagon as her father drove the horses along the road to town. When they'd arrive in the public square, he would go around to the rear of the wagon, raise his arms, and lift her down as she came sliding toward him. The color and beauty of the frontier farmer's talk flashed every once in a while in her conversation.

She had an affinity for beauty, whether practical or no.

Her books, scattered over her desk, are a mix of heavy history, fresh poetry, biography, chemistry. Unexpectedly, one comes with surprise on some small thing in her room that suggests the soul of an artist. She would hoot at the idea, but she would be pleased, because the smell of spring in the ground and the homing of flocks could never be uprooted from her life.

Grandfather Berrigan died young, on Christmas day of 1874. He suffered the dread tuberculosis; the country doctor, knowing nothing could be done, told the older girls that if severe hemorrhaging occurred they should "go outside to the rain barrel, knock out a chunk of ice, and put it in his mouth." But on that day, nothing availed, and he died, bleeding his lungs out.

She had an extraordinarily large share of what are called hard knocks. One day, in the laundry on a Saturday morning, her heart lay heavy under the burdens of being superior, principal, teacher, and plain old, all combined. So, I mentioned, which was true, that our mother provincial had said that it would be a long, long time before another like Sister Josephine would be given us. I thought she might only say "Humph" to work off her embarrassment, but she surprised me once again. She straightened up from the tub, looked me in the eye, and said, "Did she?" And her eyes were swimming with tears.

I understood, though we laughed it off, that the load presses heaviest on the thoroughbred, and all the while she was smiling and verbally sparring and amazing us all with her mischievous and quiet wit.

Our Model T was always ashine and purring on the day of the Visit Home. We collected the two sisters at the train station and proceeded homeward. The two nuns, sedate and majestical in back, one or two subdued kids up front, sandwiched in, double jeopardy, church and parent, hair plastered back, best Sunday clothes, no fooling around!

It was quite an arrival. The sisters were grandly handed down on old Main Road. The long sidewalk was crowned with a slab of granite at roadside, laid there for just such occasions in earlier times, guests alighting from high carriages. There we landed, a ritual moment, to admire the view of the lake and the shores of Solvay beyond. And by stages and easy converse, up to the house.

She told the young sisters the following story: Her superior once refused to allow her to give money to a poor woman who had come to the door. She respected the superior and had affection for her, too; but that day she was infuriated. She went around the house "wondering what this is all about." As it happened, she and the superior were to go into New York City that afternoon, to a jubilee celebration. A sumptuous dinner was served, and a sister delivered an address to the jubilarian; kept repeating, "Fifty golden years, fifty golden years . . . " And Sister Josephine, a young nun, sat like a stone, saying in her heart, "Fifty golden fiddlesticks! We couldn't give fifty coppers to a poor unfortunate."

The heat lasted for a week, and a sultry darkness.

A few years later, she was teaching at St. Stephen's in the city. And one day, she went to the door, and there was the same poor woman, and she helped her substantially.

And then, in a final twist, a neighbor told her laughingly that the "poor" woman was, in fact, rich and a fraud. . . .

To speak of her faults is to recognize a longer vision and a more fevered enthusiasm for the cause than most of us can claim.

Some felt that her strenuous life was a rebuke to the old and the sick. But her treatment of the sick sisters is a monumental story, to be told elsewhere.

She died peaceably at ninety-one in the infirmary at Mount St.

Vincent in Yonkers. The three brothers went solemnly by train to her funeral: my uncle the priest, bachelor John, and my father.

I remember how, afterward, my father wept for "the death of that beautiful mind." She did not recognize them at the end.

·4·

THE ESSAYIST

I honor in Peter Maurin a sense of tradition. Not something merely passed on hand to hand, like a palmed gem. But substance, a sanity under stress, what they call today "identity," *idem.* The person, community, faith, worship, activity in the world, all understood, carried forward, translated, part of a history of ideas, symbols, actions, modes of thought. There are recognition scenes. With a start of surprise, one comes on what one has always purportedly known. But not really known. Because the soul, life itself, is not yet colored anew, "assimilated to" in the clumsy classical phrase, the holy realities.

Tradition issues in a style. In Peter Maurin's case, the very opposite of "stylish," "relevant," a synonym for debased chic. Tradition made him an innovator; his roots made him a wanderer. That mind of his, which was so rich, so quirky, with such unexpected turns, such world savvy, so discerning—it all went along with a perfectly natural and graceful poverty. He took no more of the world than he had a right to. In that way, he lived in comparative peace on the earth—at peace with the earth.

We are coming to understand something of these things, perhaps too late. I mean the subtle interlacing of virtues, attitudes, ways of seeing and dwelling in the world, which do not curse us as an abomination on the earth. Peaceableness, poverty, the despising of stone-faced individualism, of hankering after property, of card carrying in a consumer society that is, by definition, a war-making society; and finally a cannibal society, self-destructing.

It all came out in the little prose poems, which are indeed, in style and substance, *Easy Essays.*

Did Peter mean by that that the verses would slide down the throat like a custard cream—as the instruction goes about the "little scroll" in Revelation? Did Peter mean that the essays would be "sweet as honey in the mouth, bitter as gall in the guts"?

In any case, it was a kind of "little scroll" or "little scripture" he wrote for us. Thirty-five years later, the essays stand up remarkably well. And as far as *The Catholic Worker* is concerned, their subjects and style early on set the tone of what was to come.

Literarily speaking, you could take your choice; What Peter wrote could be called poetry by the yard or prose clipped to the bone. He had come on a form as old as the prophets and the psalmist. He had also read Péguy. The abbreviated lines stop the eye in its track, get attention; repetition, key phrases, quotes, references to a huge store of authors, living and dead, classics and news stories—everything is useful and put to use, part of the whole, an argument finding its way.

He used to recite the essays, we are told, to all sorts of audiences; in those days, east to west, Catholic Workers were coming together. There were farm communities and urban parishes, college campuses, nuns and priests and a few unharnessed bishops, contemplatives and hollerers, people putting their hand to the job of starting houses where the works of mercy could come true once more. They listened and pondered and the work went on.

Peter made it two cents plain from the start: the Catholic Worker was no big deal. That was the secret. One needed only a ready hand, a few friends, a few dollars, some sense of discipline, the guts to learn as one went. The politics would rise with the bread. Houses opened, flourished; some closed, others started up. Peter grew older.

Any Catholic Worker today would recognize the rhythm. It was a *discipline* garnered from the street and from the heart. Everyone took the same vow: of instability, financially speaking. In what must be the longest-floating, free, Friday university in existence, the soul, so to speak, had *her* soup.

The rhythm continues. With, of course, an immense difference in both church and society. Peter could count on an innocent church, fascinated with its own energy and potential. Lay people, liturgy, Catholic Action, even pacifism, to a degree—the church was a bubbling pot of mysterious, savory ingredients. Eichenberg's drawings! We have a kind of CW First Supper, with Christ's back to us, the table filled with street folk, the late comer at the door.

Modern war, which broke the back of the American dream and made a stalking skeleton of the church, hardly devastated the Worker at all. Evidently, because whatever "deal" the CW had concluded was simply a covenant with the God of peace. War in consequence was small potatoes indeed, biblically speaking. It was one of those periodic spasms of empire, a sign of the end of things; more specifically, of the end of empire. As such, it was a crashing stereotype; so was its ideology, its ever-more-cunning modes of killing mind and body. No big deal! The Catholic Workers flung a kind of holy taunt at tanks and fire storms and the Bomb. People went to jail, to work camps, lost jobs, lost good repute, refused good sound money (bloodstained), refused to work in the forges and warehouses of Mars. Lost out. No big deal.

"Come down, come down!" Big Bro had to become little bro before he could be brother at all—even to his own soul. It was this deflation of big balloons that I love about Peter. He had a most unrehabilitated sense of the true human size. With it, he took the measure of Superstate—and refused worship. And in such ways, the Worker confronted war, the normal activity of the Great Stalker. War was neither to be feared nor served; successive wars became, for the Workers, simply a testing ground. Weapons, new weapons, especially those aimed at the heart of community, the heart of the mind, were tried out there and dumped: the antipersonnel weapon of untruth. Wars, and

more wars. Wars came; the church enlisted. World War II: "Yes,
but." Korea: "Perhaps . . ." Vietnam (at least in the bloody first
years): "Yes, out flat; right or wrong, yes."

But the Worker stuck fast as the great tides rolled over. Simply, unequivocally, some Christians said no. And hung on. And
were all but hanged. They were foolish and simplistic and as
intransigent as the first-generation "atheists and corruptors"
who once confounded the empire.

Did Peter foresee all this? He would have said something like:
He saw what he saw; it was enough to walk by. The essays warn
of the creeping fascism that advances under liberal and even
radical political blah; he insisted on the twinning of justice and
mercy; the war of big shots and little shots drew his ire; he saw
the slogans march and the placards drop to the gutter, the
inevitable decline from dream to burnt-out dawn. One has almost invariably the sense of a mind firmly in command of its
world, of the myths that pass for realities, the truths that starve
to death in corners and alleys of the mind. He contemned the
first, salvaged the second.

I could not put the matter too strongly. Peter, dead, was a
teacher of the sixties and seventies in a way very few among the
living were. I speak here a personal testament too precious to
assess. We had somehow to get reborn; simply, to pass from
church-as-class-phenomenon, church-as-slavey-of-empire, to
something else—church-as-noumenon, holy sign. This was
difficult beyond words. It was, in fact, when it occurred at all,
an act of God. But if it were to happen, then from a human point
of view there had to be signs along the road verifying one's
direction—also challenging one's laziness and cowardice. Signs
scornful, energizing, laconic, disruptive, reverent, attuned to
symbols and symbolic action. And plainspoken, after the "black
lung" inflicted by smoky seminary lamps.

Peter cleared the air. We breathed again.

This is by no means to lay on his bones the burden of this or
that antiwar action, taken by us or others, to this day. The point
is something other. It seems to me that Peter had a kind of
Chinese or Vietnamese sense of the unity of experience. That
was what we never heard in seminary or pulpit. Today it has the

familiar ring of a Mao dictum; but the words are Peter's: "Workers must become scholars, scholars workers." In season and out, with the unwearying patience of a sound mind, he insisted: One could never truly dwell in the world as a human until one acted on behalf of others, on behalf of life. And the act had to be grounded in that perfectly audacious sense of "tradition" that was Christ's own: "I know wherefrom I come, and where I am going. . . ." In this way, action was no mere flash in the pan, but a true epiphany of energies, undiminished in the giving, rising indeed on themselves. Coming from somewhere, therefore going somewhere.

The church Peter knew is gone, its self-confidence, innocence, optimism, bound and rebound. We have eaten of the tree, a lethal act. Whether the American church today is more than a parody of Peter's "cult, culture, cultivation" is a matter of sorrowful debate. The sense grows that it is all over; for the multitudes the cult is meaningless, the surrounding culture disintegrating, the cultivation a multicorporate grand larceny of the earth.

These are matters not merely of speculation but of considerable rancor. Was Peter ever rancorous? I think not. When I meditate uneasily on his *Easy Essays,* it seems to me that he would counsel a certain detachment. I mean from the despair that racks us, the divisions, the loss of nerve, the disappearance of landmarks. In his own day (we cannot miss it), Peter dared a great deal; he went his own way. The best of his essays do not depend on "papal social teaching" or an insistence (contested by events, many of them weirdly set in motion by a kind of curial death wish) that a "papal blueprint for society" is authentic, in a biblical sense. Peter was only rarely led down such paths; usually his sense of the church was shrewd and solid; one feels that he must have perused the gospels more carefully than he did *Osservatore Romano.*

Today he would perhaps treat Protestants more sensitively and give better attention to the plight of women, especially street folk, prisoners. Perhaps he would listen more. (Dorothy once said Peter could talk you deaf and dumb.) Still, what other Christian met the thirties and forties with the elan, lucidity, good humor, inventiveness of Peter? Or who of us here and now could predict the future, see its course as he did, let alone chart a way? The present, we say, is tormenting enough. Enough, more than enough, if we can but be faithful to, intuitive of, one or another line of that tradition that was Peter's passionate loving quest: no Ariadne's thread, but a stream followed, against the current, to its source.

In the antic circle madly celebrating the death of practically everything, loony religion, as is evident, has large part. People cannot bear the world; it is too much for addled head and undisciplined heart. Too much, let it be added, even for the clear and disciplined, quite often. With the help of nostrums and gnostics, many set about creating a world unto themselves. What a sorrowful spectacle! And how we are drawn to it, the seduction of death, the death of practically everything (and now, through the hellish ministry of the Bomb, the death of practically everyone). We cry out in anguish: Is there a single nonlunatic social structure left, in the simple sense of favoring humans, cherishing them, instructing them, a healing web of human effort, compassion, destiny? Is there, indeed, a church to turn to?

Against all the evidence, I believe there is. I think today of my friends, living and dead, at large in the minimum security of America, at small in jail. I think of Peter Maurin, of my father and mother, all that hardiness and hope, their dignity, how poor we were. How often men like Peter came knocking at the door; and men unlike Peter too, without his charm and intelligence, beaten men on the run, despair their shadow. How they were welcomed; "of a little have a little" was the working motto of those lean years. I think also how the *Easy Essays* and *The Catholic Worker* were always in the house; a penny a copy we could manage.

This was the past, which was our tradition, of which one has the right to be proud, since it is a gift, in simple fee. But I want in no sense to sound nostalgic. The test of a tradition is not that it worked for Peter or others of his generation. The question must be posed, day after day: What moral fulcrum does such a vision put to the "the world, the way it goes"? Is the vision modest, practical; does it draw us on?

I think it does. And one would like to let it go at that.

In his introduction to the 1961 revised edition of the *Easy Essays,* John Cogley said this: "The Worker had more influence on more influential Catholics than any other single force in the American church." That is a sentence I prefer to walk away from. It is, I think, a most un-Catholic Worker claim. In the spirit of the Worker, it is not merely too big a claim; it is wrong because it makes a claim at all. To paraphrase Lao-tzu, the biggest sunflower in the world doesn't know it. When it learns it, it already has a price on its head. Who said existence and life were competitive anyway?

Thank God, then, for this centenary, this Christian. And for Dorothy. And for those who, in the fifties, refused to take shelter against the nuclear storms—a gimmick of mother state on the one hand, a grace of mother church on the other.

Thank God for the constancy of those who never bought the latest war, which was supposed to be a good war because it was our war, just war, holy war, safe war, sound war. No, it was a bad war no matter what; because it was war. Thank you.

For the draft resisters—of the forties, fifties, sixties, seventies, eighties. All those flaming cards of nonidentity, of amnesia, of unholy obedience, those hunting licenses against humans! Oh, what a savory smoke their burning set off, what a light they shed, once they were no more!

And for the trade unionists. And the teachers. The mothers and fathers. Those who opened houses and maintained them along with their families, in poverty oftener than not, and insecurity, and illness.

For that humming wire of moral continuity, incandescent and burning. The message got through, even to the tardy, even to us: It is not allowed to kill one another; it is incumbent on us to feed, clothe, cherish one another.

For my parents, who dug deep, as did Peter. These were compatible spirits; they would have recognized one another. Indeed, I believe they did, in many strange and rich ways, in "the breaking of the bread."

Peter, thank you. Indeed, you started something.

· 5 ·

THE WOMAN

Dorothy Day's pilgrimage must surely be accounted an extraordinary life and accomplishment.

Writing as I do shortly after her death, any evaluation must be modest and tentative; the gestation of her memory is barely under way. Yet her place in the history of the century would seem already secure. It begins with those who loved her, lived with her, worked and wept with her, and both feared and faced her death. With them, as with thousands of others, there could be no doubt that Dorothy now belongs to history—as exemplar, mystic, lover of life, fighter of the good fight.

She is gone from us; the work of iconography so stoutly resisted by her (and her church) can get under way. As can those cooler and equally important evaluations of Dorothy from the point of view of culture, political aspiration, sociology, secular ethic. In this respect she was much like her great friends Merton and Maurin; she can be understood only as a Catholic Christian. But unlike them, she was no cosmopolite; her grip was on the American idiom and style and mental workings, the continental insularity, both liberating, and petrifying, of this country; it seems fair to say that such a phenomenon as Dorothy Day could have burst on no other scene than ours.

More of this later. But in calling her American to the marrow,

I am not thinking merely of her marxist idealism, her pragmatism, the way she exasperated ideologues and gurus by joining issues to lives, her passion for freedom to the point of waywardness, her star performance in the jungle market of journalism, her life of gyrovague, disturber of mordant peace. Her sense of being daughter of this time and place went beyond; it brought her into the Catholic church.

There she found the basis, ground, for her adversary style: the signs, the "social doctrine," the ideology, the sacred she so yearned for, transfiguring the struggle, giving it scope, purpose, a final day. She found, so to speak, the Book from whose pages, warnings, frowns, threats, promise she could look up and shout aloud, in terror, anger, justice outraged.

In Catholicism she came not so much to her own place (too static a term), but to her true self, in natural setting—and motion. Herself, embattled. But never alone, never for once deprived of a "cloud of witnesses." A struggle now against forces clearly identified, a longer more enlightening history of life as drama; all this, and a larger vista of hope. She wrote that she had nothing to regret or leave behind in becoming a Christian. It was a strange, wonderful statement, for she had indeed lost much. But what she had lost (her lover and friend) she measured against all she had gained; a terrible beauty was born. And perhaps in such a disclaimer she was thinking not so much of her great renunciation as of the feckless, bohemian episodes that preceded it. In any case, all that is done with.

Those of us who knew her only in her later years were tempted, I think, to regard her rather thoughtlessly. That is, we saw her as a phenomenal presence whose greatness and goodness had descended full blown in our midst, easily won and as easily dispensed abroad. She seemed always to have been as she was: serene, graced with her aura of piety and pity.

Perhaps this sense of her, wrong as it was, was inevitable. For she was the soul of reticence about her past—or, indeed, about her present estate. Except for a few revealing passages in *The Long Loneliness,* her brisk mind was at home, so to speak, outside itself. Her ordinary grist was the stuff of life: work, faith, friends, hope, the poor, rent and food, work strikes, cupidity and injustice, and above all the skeletal leer of war mocking our days and nights. These were the rub, the horror and hope—of her life, of the lives of those who wished to join up and walk to her beat. These must be argued through, acted upon. She banged out her praxis on kitchen tables, in buses, before audiences of every kind, in every corner of the land.

An American woman came of an American family; a touch, no more, of Eugene O'Neill or Arthur Miller. In Dorothy's childhood, Day senior roamed the country, East Coast to West, someone called a "newsman," perpetually on the spoor of something called a "story." Whatever it was, it was to make their fortune. It was the quintessential American dream; the children were caught up in it—a hit-and-miss education, fat days and lean, life on the road. And amid it all, drinking it in, this wideeyed, intensely observant child.

It was a good family, recalled with affection. The parents were never dull or demeaning: warm at the center, a bit chilly at the edges. The child loved books, read like a demon: Jack London, Kropotkin, Upton Sinclair, Frank Harris on the Haymarket anarchists, Vincent Sheean, Eugene Debs. There was an infant brother whom she loved boundlessly. All considered, hers was a lucky start. She tasted love, a first taste of nature.

Her first crisis was a religious one. She tells it vividly, as though turning a single page, a memory thin as membrane. On the one hand, she was studying everything from the anarchist history of America to the New Testament, a regime unrefined and chaotic.

Then she would look outward, into her poor Chicago neighborhood. She saw violence, injustice, strikes, police flailing away, political martyrs. She saw America: a brutalizing, defacing, death-dealing machine. Many years later she was to refer to it in disgust and anger as "this filthy rotten system."

She read Jesus' words, the words of the early disciples, found them dovetailing her vision of the way the world should go. She looked for Christians, and she saw something else. The Christians were like everyone else.

In recoil, one thinks, she joined the Socialist party in her first year of college.

Children look at things very directly and simply. I did not see anyone taking off his coat and giving it to the poor. I didn't see anyone having a banquet and calling in the lame, the halt and the blind. . . . I wanted, though I did not know it then, a synthesis. I wanted life and I wanted the abundant life. I wanted it for others too. . . . I wanted everyone to be kind. I wanted every home to be open to the lame, the halt and the blind. . . .

Only then did people really live, really love their brothers. In such love was the abundant life, and I did not have the slightest idea how to find it.

She is now a college student, winner of a scholarship. She is reaching out, for affection, concordance of minds. She has also undergone a kind of preconversion; and though she is nowhere within shouting distance of the church, she has taken its measure, she knows where to find it. She knows what the church looks like; or, infinitely more to the point, she knows what it should look like.

There is a mutuality here worthy of note. What the church is, or will be, to her is analogous to what she is, or will be, to the church. I mean something extremely simple. When Dorothy enters its portals, the American church will undergo momentous changes, as though at a signal, a trumpet blast from a baroque ceiling. She will speak of Peter Maurin, her friend and mentor, as a "one-man revolution." But we are not to be fooled; there is a slight correction to be made. The revolution was in fact hers, a woman's. It was she who grounded Peter's lightnings, in long travail and patience, in planning and scrimping, she who got the Catholic Worker houses going and kept them going, who instructed and guided the young, bore with the foolish and ne'er-do-wells.

It was she who kept insisting: There is no mercy without justice. Kept insisting: The most dreadful injustice of the modern world is the crime of war.

It is here, I would judge, we touch on her great gift to the church. She saw the world wobbling perilously; its axis was the tip of a blade. The hand holding the sword that upheld the world, that whirled it crazily, belonged to a very ape of God. It was the hand of Mars, god of death. And until he was deprived of his prey, not by political means or military means, but by the hands of the Crucified, the world would never again move in its proper orbit and light. It would fall, literally and from grace.

Further, the saving hands must be our own, the hands of believers. Thus, she restored to our hands their proper function and anointing. But this was far in the future.

> I was happy as a lark at leaving home. I was sixteen and filled with a great sense of independence. I was on my own, and no longer to be cared for by the family. . . . It was experience in general that I wanted. I did not think in terms of philosophy or sociology. I continued the same courses I had been taking, Latin, English, history and science. . . .

She was, as she tells, quite pragmatic about college, and is unabashed in the telling. She lazed about, soaking up her neighborhood, skipped classes that held no interest, seemed to find in friendship her real awakening. Officially speaking, she turned in a tolerable performance; but like so many of her tribe (who were to make of her style a hallmark of a later decade), she kept her distance from straight academe; worked, so to speak, her own side of the street.

Then she came to New York, and the second broad phase of her life got under way. She began work as a newspaper woman, much in the way of Emma Goldman, a liberal among the Greenwich Village playwrights and poets. She moved among bohemians, serious artists, workers, theorists, parasites.

To Dorothy it was as though she were shot from the mouth of a cannon. From a relatively staid and sequestered campus of the Midwest, she was thrust into a volcano: O'Neill, Eastman, *The Masses,* Terry Carlin, Michael Gold. "No one ever wanted to go to bed," she writes (surely a hyperbole) "and no one ever wished to be alone."

With her suffragist friends she took to the streets of Washington and was arrested. That time, the ordeal was relatively brief. The second arrest was a different matter entirely, a taste of savage American justice, involving a hunger strike and a punishment cell.

She did a year's stint as a nurse at King's County Hospital. Then she left for an extended stay in Europe (with whom and for how long she does not say). She passes that year over with the cryptic remark that, after all, she never intended to write an autobiography, but only to "tell of the things that brought me to God and that remind me of God." Evidently her trip, and her companion, did neither.

Her state of soul at the time remains a puzzle—most of all, one senses, to herself. She oscillates between disbelief and—something, a country dimly perceived, then lost to her, a mirage. In yet another mood she draws apart in some church; but the stillness is a pit; she sits there trapped. Where does she belong, what is she to do with her life?

Hers was, among other things, a crisis of imbalances, of gifts misused, neglected, taken for granted. She was a person of great stamina, carrying a load that she shifted from right hand to left, but never without deep discomfort, a sense of being off center. How is she to manage her journey less painfully, how attain balance? She can perhaps carry everything on her head, or on her back—or in her heart. She could drag her possessions, gifts, insights, the pain of the world, behind her. But these are temporary appeasements, respites. She tried them all. And each and all, after a time, were unavailing. Everything of her life, her loves, skills, writings, friendships, family, social passion—things she admired and envied in others, emoluments, radiances, gifts —in her hands they turned to stone.

For all her reticence, the suffering of those years comes through, a suffering that soured the honey of life. By any worldly standard, which is to say, by any standard available to her and her circle, her life was all success and solid achievement. Who could fault her? She had courage, a sharp mind, a tongue to match. She had nursed the ill in a great urban hospital, worked on the staff of respected papers. She had been arrested and jailed, the ultimate honor among her kind. And so on, and so on. What more was she asking of life?

The man I loved, with whom I entered into a common law

marriage, was an anarchist, an Englishman by descent, and a biologist.

This was the "more." After much tumult and storms that never seemed to clear, Dorothy's life touches shore, "out of the arm of the sea." Her prose grows idyllic, characters wander in and out, hilarious, feckless friends, unclassifiable fauna of sea and land, crawling, sidling, running to her side. The figure is doubly tempting, since she and her lover set up a rickety household on the Staten Island shore. There the tides, moon changes, days and nights washed ashore practically anyone imaginable. She has total, vivid recall. The island saga is perhaps the most detailed and delightful period of her life, as the woman of mid-fifties recalls the woman of twenty-four. Forster is by no means her first love, but he is the last, all that matters. Sasha, Freda, the beachcomber Lefty and his lobster pot, the leaky old cottage bobbing in autumn storms like a badly anchored buoy, Peggy Cowley and her furs and cosmos and "highbred nose," Dorothy supporting herself and her lover by pounding out potboilers; the hilarity and innocence, the pearly glow before the dark, before the dawn; something of both, something beyond either. Dorothy conceived a child.

It was the child's birth, she says, that brought her faith to term. An old story but a new one, too. She was to develop it masterfully, not only in the pages of her "nonautobiography," but in *New Masses,* for which she wrote an account of Tamar's birth that was to become a classic.

The baby was born; it must be baptized. The imperative lay as strong on her as the child had weighed within her. And immediately another crisis was under way. She was already, at least in spirit, a Catholic; the child would shortly be baptized in the church. And her lover, the father of her child, came down hard; he was irrevocably opposed to religion: hers, the child's, anyone's.

The wonder here is not that Forster, enigmatic, solitary, watery dreamer, ineffectual pure spirit, who despised, distanced himself not only from the tin-can culture of America, but from any attempt to clean up the social debris—the wonder is not that he stood against the Catholicism of that day. As a measure of his world, an expression of its logic, ethos, conscience, concordance with the evidence available (an evidence by no means exciting or evangelical), his animus, his sense of loss and pain and resentment—all these make considerable sense.

He raised very hell with her purpose. And his anger had a deeper source than an infant's baptism; he was intelligent enough to sense that things would by no means stop there, an aspersion cast over a child. The mother who thrust the infant into magic and the unknown would surely and shortly follow. And how right was his instinct, in more ways than one.

I think of this man, this survivor, the one left out, the one from whom, like a Graham Greene protagonist, she must tear heart and destiny and child. Her decision to convert cut clean as a death stroke; not only her death, but his as well. A double indemnity it must have been: Catholicism laying claim to her, and just as ruthlessly disclaiming him.

She read the words of Jesus, austere and uncompromising, concerning a faith that sunders families, breaks blood ties, violates nature at its marrow. All for the sake of a higher calling, the call of Christ, arranger and wrecker of lives. She heard the call, and Forster did not. And, in justice, it must be added that the voice of Christ, summoning her to leave her lover and friend, was filtered through a "law of the church," which she, with every fiber of her soul, identified with the voice of the gospel harrower.

In another time, after Vatican II, one is led to speculate on a far different outcome. Need their tie have been broken so cruelly, her beloved set adrift?

In any case, Dorothy stated simply and finally the choice before her, a choice that at that time, and according to her lights and the law, allowed of no leeway.

> To become a Catholic meant for me to give up a mate with whom I was much in love. It got to the point where it was the simple question of whether I chose God or man.

The decision entered her being. For the rest of her life, it colored her attitude toward marriage, remarriage, divorce, sexual conduct—and the church. A time would come when priests and religious would marry, despite the law, when lay men and women would divorce and seek other partners. In every case her reaction was unyielding; her crisis, its cost, welled up. If she (and he?) had made a choice that by every criterion must be accounted heroic, why was less to be expected of other Catholics, at any time, under whatever impulse?

On social issues she was a furious innovator. She found the church a tabula rasa, and with great pain and the controlled nicety of genius, she inscribed the texts, lost or defaced or simply erased by cultural banality: Thou shall not kill. Turn the other cheek. Walk a second mile. . . .

And all the while, in matters sexual and marital, she conserved, controlled, broke friendships, tossed free-loving hippies out on their ears, forbade Catholic deviants access to her paper. A tempting analogy occurs: When the chips were down, Tamar was *her* child, not Forster's and hers. And when other chips were down, *The Catholic Worker* was *her* paper, not hers and the other editors'. There on the masthead stood the redoubtable words for some thirty-five years: Publisher and Editor, Dorothy Day.

Only after a long time did she give place once more to her native tenderness. In old age, she began to inquire with feeling about those she had once loved and named her friends, then written off. She confided that she was visiting her husband, now old and ill, in hospital. She inquired after Philip and Elizabeth and others, wrote them letters, sought news of the children.

Her Catholic conversion remains a wondrous mystery. Why did Dorothy, in the maturity of her gifts, rejoicing in the fruition of her body, why did this agnostic and anarchist, veteran of jails, marches, fasts for justice, soul mate of a man who was, as she confessed, the very half of her soul, the Dorothy of strikes and prisoners and the condemned of the earth, this woman whose natural habitat was the underworld of the victims, the excluded, the urban poor, this woman so sensual, worldly wise—why did she renounce, against all sound reason, her only love, cut her past, anger and bewilder her friends?

She did this momentous thing, and more. She cast her fate, not toward some fashionable creed, one of worldly promise, a church vibrant with social passion, whose flame would invigorate and intensify her own. By no means such a church.

Nonetheless, she converted. Because—she believed. If the statement is illogical, so much the worse. So was she. She became a child again. An aged, rather ignorant nun was her instructor. Dorothy's memory stuck in its groove; sister's tongue often descended like a ferule, as the neophyte struggled to give back by rote the uncompromising truths of Baltimore Catechism Number One.

And Dorothy cannot believe her good fortune. Her head swims with the glory of it all, the gift. By anticipation she meets the objections of her friends. She is certainly not led by unhappiness into the church; indeed, she is in a very stupor of joy for having borne her child. Nor is Christ, she writes, a panacea against the travails and emptiness of the world.

> I wanted to die in order to live, to put off the old man and put on Christ. I loved, in other words, and like all women in love, I wanted to be united to my love. . . .
> I loved the church for Christ made visible. Not for itself, because it was so often a scandal to me. . . . There was plenty of charity but too little justice.

Did she enter the church like a queen a hovel, gracing its squalor and ignorance with her radiant intelligence, her noble sensibility, her passion to set the world right? Did she enter, lamp in hand, crowned with her gifts, crowned above all with the grace of a great denial? The image is a tempting one; it has much to commend it. Except that it is a violation of her sense of herself.

Let others see her in somewhat this way, understanding as they must that this is by no means the way she saw herself. Her conduct bespeaks a far different image. What one can only call, for lack of better words, humility, a sense of rightful place and scope; what Paul Goodman names "creatureliness." And with respect to the church, a sense of having entered a mystery infinitely surpassing human gifts, talents, grasp of reality. This is her tone, her style; it is fraught with ironies, humor, grim conflict. She bows before the priest; she acknowledges his power over the invisible. But she reserves to herself the right to excoriate the church for playing whore, Judas, Cain; for playing the worldly game of power and money and institutional glory.

These are the ironies she both embraces and helps create and intensify. And withal, in her style and tone, she is herself, as she always has been. Her distinction and dignity are drawn from poverty, not possessions. She wears plain cotton dresses chosen, like any poor woman's, from the racks of hand-me-downs. There is a faded kerchief about her crown of hair. Her language is direct and lucid, utterly free of pietism. Her heart is unresting as ever; compassion racks her frame.

So the future hovers, an eyelid upon an eye, half-closed against too great a light. The worst is over; she has made a clean break, has reached a haven.

And now what? She went one day, in the course of a news assignment in Washington, into a shrine to pray. Her prayer, she tells us, was disarmingly specific. She wanted someone to cross her path, which was, she mourned, no path at all, but a stalemate. She prayed for someone to enter her life, to show her a way.

And thereupon she returned to New York, to her apartment. And there, a doppelganger, an unlikely answer taking shape before her, stood, or sat, or ambled about (the accounts vary)— one Peter Maurin.

And now her true life gets under way. Peter struck a match to her combustible heart. He offered her both a theory and a persuasive and patient example, a Christianity at once worldly, matter-of-fact, intensely personal, a method and means. Peter was what might be called today, in the best sense of that mutilated term, an evangelical. Which is to say, he took the intent of Christ seriously: the neighbor, the call to labor and sacrifice, the drudgery that made the kingdom possible.

Indeed, though Peter was twenty years her senior, the main outlines of his life had run parallel to her own, in a quite startling way. By temperament and grace and sheer dogged will, he was fitted for the great work he had set himself. And so, as he sized up this neophyte, as he was to insist day in and out, so was she. Or if she was not, if she doubted herself, he would so fit her.

Which he proceeded to do, with a persistence at once fascinating and irritating. He declared that her education was deficient in Catholic understanding. But it was not too late, since he, Peter, was at hand and would correct the defect. He would introduce her to the great thinkers of the century, and beyond: Mauriac, Maritain, Gilson, Péguy, Dostoievski, the social writings of the popes. He would elaborate this doctrine, synthesize it, for her and others.

This hardy tumbleweed, blown hither and yon by the winds of the spirit, finally lodged in her door. Peter was at the mercy of those winds, which also had their eye, a center of mystery, a peasant's faith. What a man he was! She groaned and gloried. If a saint were to appear in her lifetime, would it not be in some such guise as Peter's, the truth bursting from his seams, the word ready on his tongue, no fear, no second thoughts, only that hardy, single-minded frame of obscurity and poverty, speaking the truth for the truth's sake?

How alike they were, Dorothy and Peter, and how complementary. A similar genius, at once dogged and rugged, a grasp of essentials, a linking of theory and practical love. Peter knew the world, a world of blind waste and want and war. And he remained serene, unafflicted by fatalism. Granted the evil, it was a world to be won; people need not die as they had lived, the world of salvation, the daily bread, all were at hand. And this was the task: Bread and truth must make the rounds.

He taught her to look on the world this way. Bread and truth, truth and bread, making the rounds. Today's food would yield, short of death (the death of the soul), to tomorrow's hunger; the task would never end. But let tomorrow take care of itself; it was today's hunger that must be met. Let us meet it. Let us multiply ourselves, in the youth, the workers, the poor, the street people, the excluded. All have the truth to offer; all can multiply the bread, bake it, break it, pass it on.

They started a newspaper; and the rest is history.

They started a house of hospitality; that too is history. Peter was forever talking about something he called "agronomic universities." They started one, on the land; and that is something rather less than history.

The paper grew like mad. Peter's timing, and Dorothy's as well, was impeccable. Not all American Catholics, it developed, were wired to a party line. Not all priests; wonderfully, not all bishops. The depression, the Spanish war, World War II swept over the flock, brimstone and cloudbursts. The sheep were rattled and voiceless, surcharged with discipline and dogma, fed windily on abstraction. And downwind sailed an omen and land-ed at their feet: this cheaply printed broadsheet, bold, uncom-promising, reminiscent of something outrageous and familiar at once, black on white, a penny a copy. Month after month, through thick and thin, take it or leave; proworker, antiwar, prostrikers and prisoners and the down and out. Drawings by Eichenberg, Ade Bethune, Rita Corbin; art bold as a sandwich board, a clamor of forms, figures rough-hewn, stature and sanc-tity. And here and there and everywhere, within the crude art and text, like honey in a dead jaw bone, dwelt an enormous tenderness and compassion.

Dorothy was in her glory. She had found a master, a way. Peter? He had found a disciple worthy of his mettle.

Disciple, master; an interesting arrangement; but, to right thinking, one to be dispensed with as soon as might be. A rule, one might add, not universally honored in that time or ours.

In Dorothy's case, the rule was upheld—to the honor of both parties. There came a day, the date by no means certain, when Peter was no longer master, Dorothy no longer neophyte. Dorothy had begun to see things with her own eyes, judge with her own mind. And more, on occasion she judged differently than Peter; and he, having stated his case, accepted her judg-ment.

Dorothy tells the story, without dwelling on its implications, or perhaps even grasping them. Twice, she tells us, Peter was ready to give up. Once, when opposition had arisen against their using slim resources to feed the poor. The money, so the objection went, was better spent for propaganda, printing, and the support of editors of the paper. The language of the young

Turks was interestingly, and typically, loaded: Substance was being wasted on "bums, derelicts, dead wood."

And Peter could bear it no longer. He stood up, beckoned to Dorothy: "Come, let us leave the house and paper to them." And she sat there, not budging. The tempest passed; so did the malcontents, who left to start their own paper on their own turf. Which shortly thereafter folded.

On another occasion, Peter was shaken by the outcry against their pacifist stand. "Perhaps," he confessed, "it is time to be silent; they are not willing to listen." And, again, Dorothy withstood him. Granted a hearing or lost on the wind, the truth must be spoken. In season and out. Hot war and cold, false peace and true. In face of the deadly drum beat of the nations, the wars crowding one after another like bloody lock-stepping squads—no matter. *The Catholic Worker* must go on, in her words, "opposing war and upholding the stand of the conscientious objector, and the absolutist who advocated non payment of taxes and nonregistration. . . ."

It was a dead-serious game; she was playing Paul to her Peter, "withstanding him to his face."

I am led to reflect, without attempting to blow the matter out of proportion, how often the coherence of a social movement, its moral substance, the possibility of offering an example to the immature, even the unborn—how often the chancy future rests on such moments, such speaking up. Seizing the occasion, not only to vindicate a truth here and now, but to guarantee as far as one can (it is not very far) a decent outcome.

How stunningly right she was to hang on, to endure. And yet she did not know if she was right or wrong and confesses to nagging thoughts:

> Peter may have been right on both occasions, silence may have been better. . . . But I do not know. God gives us our temperaments, and in spite of my pacifism, it is natural for me to stand my ground, to continue in what actually amounts to a class war, using such weapons as the works of mercy for immediate means to show our love and to alleviate suffering.

This strikes me as a triumph, modest, but a triumph nonetheless. The dove devouring the serpent.

I am conscious, too, of a kind of relief, perhaps mingled with selfishness; of gratitude also, remembering all that Dorothy's "withstanding" has meant to me and mine. When William Miller's history of *The Catholic Worker* was published, I had just come out of prison during the Vietnam years. I stayed up all night, unable to put the book aside. What held me in thrall was an absolutely stunning consistency. No to all killing. Excusing causes, invasions, incursions, call of the blood, summonings to the bloody flag, casuistic body counts; just wars, necessary wars, religious wars, needful wars, holy wars—into the teeth of the murderous crosswinds went her simple word. *No.*

Thus a large matter arose out of small, like a great and growing pyramid, reversed, steady on its apex. If Dorothy learned anything from Peter, even by opposing him, it was the power of that single monosyllable, turning her away from every enticement to compromise, to come to terms, to make it big, to institutionalize, to play god, to cotton up to the monied and powerful.

It was an unforgettable example; some of us never forgot it.

A moral premise had been examined, discussed, held up to light and darkness, exposed to public and ecclesiastical scrutiny, undergone objection and obloquy even—then a fully formed, conscientious position emerged, a light to a whole generation.

Her no to war was ultimately as simple as a newborn lisp. But it came out of much travail and searching and converging experience. In this, as in all serious matters, Dorothy took the long route to the center. Somewhat in this way. She resolved to taste the violence of American life, dreadfully apparent in marginal and expendable people. She would become, like Peter before her, a kind of holy *vaga*, a wandering scholar and worker. Thus the stigmata of her people dug deep in her hands and soul. She came to see that, in America, human devastation was by no means fortuitous; it was embedded in the scheme and texture and finality of the social contract, like rods of steel reinforcing, prestressing the dead weight of life.

One scholar, a refugee and former prisoner, queried her,

"How close are you to the workers?" It was, she said, a pertinent question; and she answered it with a lifting pride:

> Going around and seeing such sights is not enough. To help the organizers, to give what you have for relief, to pledge yourself to voluntary poverty for life so that you can share with your brothers is not enough. One must live with them, share with them their sufferings too. Give up one's privacy, and mental and spiritual comforts as well as physical. . . .
>
> Yes, we have lived with the poor, with the workers, and we know them not just from the streets, or in mass meetings, but from years of living in the slums, in tenements, in our hospices in Washington, Baltimore, Philadelphia, Harrisburg, Pittsburgh, New York, Rochester, Boston, Worcester, Buffalo, Troy, Detroit, Cleveland, Toledo, Akron, St. Louis, Chicago, Milwaukee, Minneapolis, Seattle, San Francisco, Los Angeles, Oakland, even down into Houma, Louisiana. . . .
>
> We have lived with the unemployed, the sick, the unemployables. . . . Going to the people is the purest and best act in Christian tradition and is the beginning of world brotherhood. . . .

A mystic, she was blessed and burdened with a very thirst for reality. But the prior synthetic gift is withheld from her (another mark of her American soul). She had to see and touch and listen—and then cry out. She had perpetually to be "on the road." The country was seething with anguish and discontent; it was, as she said wearily, "always something": strikes or unemployment or war or the dispossession of those on the land, or civil rights crises. She had to be on hand, protesting such evils, going to jail.

And hers was a further burden: She must report back to her readers, the beloved "larger family" of *The Catholic Worker.* They winged it along with her; they saw America through the courage and vision that bore her along.

"On Pilgrimage" became her letter to the world, a column that ran for some thirty years in her paper, up to the month of her death. She wrote from Cuba, from Rome, from jail, from the farm fields of migrant workers, from coal-mining areas, from the reservations of the West. In her travels, she lived with, talked with, ate with, walked miles with, marched with; she became the guardian angel of the unangelic, a very angel of "with." It was her way, as she announced, literal as ever, of not separating Jesus from his cross.

In the course of a bitter winter in the early seventies, a group of California farm workers crossed the country in an unheated coffin of a van. They were hoping to undertake a grape boycott on the East Coast. They arrived in New York and showed up promptly at the Catholic Worker. Dorothy received them like long-lost brothers. And it was there, on the first floor of East First Street, as I arrived to offer mass on a cold February day, that I and others first met the people of Cesar Chavez and his movement. Dorothy introduced the knot of dark, apparently unthawed folk, huddled on benches along the wall. Above them hung a new symbol, the farm workers' flag, black eagle on red; it has hung there ever since.

Meantime, Dorothy had written about, defended, explained the following: cotton pickers, braceros, prisoners and ex-prisoners, families of every condition, the unemployed, priests and nuns, scholars, Native Americans, monks, alcoholics, addicts, slum folk, auto workers, coal miners. Among others.

She stood with them. In the current jargon, and venturing the understatement of the century, she had "a point of view." She had long before recovered from the malaise of her profession, which she described more properly as its curse: the inability to sort things out, the reeling head, the condensed brain, the eye that, seeing everything, sees nothing. She became, that is, a reporter with a conscience—a phenomenon that daily grows rarer.

The Vietnam war erupted. Dorothy stood at the side of those who refused to "serve," which is to say (as she would say) refused to kill.

I well remember the first draft-card burning. We arranged for a mass at the apartment of one of the men who was resolved to put the torch to his odious hunting license. I was permitted by superiors to lead the mass, but not to appear in company with potential felons in Union Square (the kind of order that was corrected, in measure, as the war went on). Dorothy saw the young Workers go off to court and jail; she was proud as a mother of heroes; they were doing the truest "alternative service," she declared. She wrote of them and their wives, praised their courage, pledged that the Catholic Worker would sustain the separated families.

Our best and truest memories are invariably suffused with gratitude. I am grateful beyond words for the grace of this woman's life; for her sensible, unflinching rightness of mind, her long and lonely truth, her journey to the heart of things. I think of her as one who simply helped us, in a time of self-inflicted blindness, to see.

At length all was said and done; no more needed saying and doing. So she stood there, or sat down, like Christ, like the Buddha. This is the image of her last years. Her life passed over, into passive voice. Now she was served, reverenced, cherished, protected. Her flame was failing; her memory glimmered and guttered; "On Pilgrimage" became a barely audible murmur of space and silence as she struggled to say her farewell to the world.

I dare speak finally for eight Christians, the Plowshare defendants. The best tribute we could offer Dorothy is that we too would stand somewhere, or sit down. In any case, somewhere. In any case, in trouble. In our case, indicted, tried, convicted, and jailed for having destroyed, in September 1980, in King of Prussia, Pennsylvania, two nuclear warheads. It was the first nuclear disarmament, we proudly proclaimed, in thirty-five years. Without Dorothy, without that exemplary patience, courage, moral modesty, without this woman pounding at the locked door behind which the powerful mock the powerless with games of triage—without her, the resistance we have offered would be simply unthinkable. She urged our consciences off the beaten track; she made the impossible (in our case) probable, and then actual. She did this, first of all, by living as though the truth were true.

All honor to you, Dorothy! You dwell now in that place where the revolution has come true, perpetually renewed, perennially green.

Be with us, in our saying and doing. In our standing somewhere and our sitting down.

THE JESUIT

> While a passionate age storms ahead, setting up new things
> and tearing down old, raising and demolishing as it goes, a
> reflective and passionless age does exactly the contrary. It
> hinders and stifles all action. It levels. . . .
> Enthusiasm may indeed end in disaster, but leveling is eo ipso
> the destruction of the individual. No age, and therefore not
> the present age, can bring the scepticism of that process to a
> halt. For as soon as it tries, the law of the leveling process is
> again brought into play. Leveling can only be halted by the
> individual attaining the religious courage which springs from
> his individual religious solitude.
>
> (Kierkegaard, *The Present Age*)

The episode had all the wacked-out improbability of a grade-
C, dog-day movie. Indeed, a furious, illiterate enemy of Rome
could have done no worse. Take one learned and passionate
Jesuit out on a limb; take an obscure Roman cardinal armed
with a snickersnee; interpose one embattled Jesuit general abet-
ting said cardinal. Down comes limb, Jesuit, passion, and all.

We thought, really, we had done with all that. Vatican II had
solemnized the resolve; Pope John had given over his short and
happy life to the prospect. Never again secret character assassi-

nations secretly arrived at; no more suffocations, immurations, exiles, dismissals, enforced silencings; no more midnight burials at crossroads; no more stakes through the heart of prophetic purpose. We had done with all that. We were to become, shortly and radically, a new sort of spectacle unto the world. Behold, in our midst no more macho or macha, Jew or gentile, homo or hetero. One holy, indivisible, color-blind, age-blind, sex-blind. Authority in service, symbol and reality, rite and follow-through, one seamless conscience, one body of love.

The documents went bravely about it; they were a raiment of poverty decked in ribbons for a holiday, our baptismal robe. We would do what we had purposed to do; it was simple as that. The will was the grace; the grace blessed the performance. We were canceling out the evil in our history, taking a new turn, indeed rising from the dead. The Bible was coming alive in us. Once and for all, the new community was to be born, sprung, mature and purposeful, ready for passion and action in the world.

It was a little like the heady romanticism that bubbled up in American society in the sixties. Everything was possible to us, even a reborn culture; even (God help us) the rebirth of political arrangement. We would turn everything over, we would turn out all the rascals, we would begin anew.

Such a fever of anticipated triumph! It swept everything before it—for a while. It lived along the wave like an ecstatic surfer. Impossible to fail, only watch us!

Alas, the wave subsided; the surfer went under, head over heels. In Kierkegaard's phrase, the Passionate Age was succeeded by the Great Leveler.

A new tactic is thereupon called for. Mere prudence, a sense of survival, dictate that, in the age of leveling, one keep a low profile. Lest one be leveled. The principle is honored in anthropology, under some rubric like "The Law of Survival." The same law has much to say to experts in other fields. (Not to speak of simple folk who would prefer, by and large, to survive until sundown.) Money makers know how to lie low when a bullish market goes sluggish. Politicians learn the difference between an open and an off season on speaking up, the difference between a good but bootless issue versus a juicy if spurious one; when to push and pull, when to rock gently with the grain. Roman churchmen? They are masters of the shifts and tides of this world. Their fifth gospel, like a fifth wheel, is always ready, in case, just in case. (The other four may or may not do; one cannot be sure.) This one is named Sweet Reason. Or the Lesser Evil. Or the Greater Good. In any case, Assembled in Italy.

The point of all this is to suggest a contrast. On the one hand, the Levelers. On the other, the out-of-tune, out-of-joint, out-of-step character named by Kierkegaard "the religious individual." This one has no sense of right timing, cannot read traffic signs, has indeed no interest in reading them, is utterly and incurably irrelevant (to all but one thing), speaks up when everyone urges equivocal prudence, is silent in the midst of hot contention, has no authority beyond the useless currency of human concern. He (she) has only the simplest of projects to commend him: a project that arose from walking in the world and observing events there. It might be put like this: to save or aid one other person, or a few. The project, of course, makes little sense in an age leveled off to hot crowds and shifty crowd pleasers.

In any case, our religious individual is the very opposite of a stereotype, even of a stereotype Jesuit. That vocation, peculiar in nature, is popularly supposed to call one out of the crowd to become a crowd pleaser (albeit capable of sternness at times, with a nice critical edge). This character, it is said, niftily redeems the times by going with the times, not against them; an optimist to the core, a "redemptive" optimist, just to get the language straight. What this comes down to is an old skill first outlined by Socrates: a Jesuit, they say, can make the worse argument appear the better, whenever the worse argument redounds to a measure of corporate benefit. (What's good for one of Ours is good for all of Ours.) He has, moreover, no hesitation in embracing what is culturally meretricious. (Even the enemy would admit this is rare; though the Jesuits might admit it is too unrare for comfort.) The tactic here being political clout in harness to rampageous ego, as in the case of McLaughlin huckstering Nixon's war. Or perhaps a silly enchantment with mass-media frenzy, as in the concocters of *The Exorcist*. But these, I am relieved to report, are instances of Ours at their determined worst. And when we are lucky, as in the outcome of the above lamentable grotesqueries, the agents do their little (or large) worst and pass from the scene, chastened or defiant as the case may be, but on their own.

The stereotype is the exception in real life. And this is what gives us hope; there are Jesuits and Jesuits. There are Enthusiasts and Levelers; there are Icemen and Firemen, Indians and Chiefs, Manicurists and Sore Thumbs.

The latter is the burden of these reflections. For it is the Sore Thumb that tells us the condition of the body. And, to that degree, the pain of one member is to the honor of all, a sign to be winced at. We have had, in these last unamiable years, some ten thumbs on our two American hands, all of them both clumsy and sore, a redundancy of pain. Something is indeed wrong; but then, at least a wrong is given us to know, and with a vengeance.

One Jesuit lately held up his pain (and ours) before the befuddled public gaze, a gaze that quickly, in official eye sockets, has darkened with horror. Consider the case. A Doctor of Philosophy in the time-honored mold, teacher, writer, counselor. To this point, no pain; all well and good. I met John McNeil years ago, in Europe. He was undergoing the grueling obstacle race *honoris causa* at Louvain. Our paths crossed briefly, as I recall, in Paris. We got on well. He was amiable and alive in the mind; certainly we were both great innocents, with the dreadful, uncharted future lying out there, and we bemused, thinking our lives would go straight as the arrow of God's (purported) will: safe, sound, bell, book, candle, cassock, rule, long black line, classroom, rec room, womb-to-tomb security.

It's all gone, for good; in more senses than one. Now he's grizzled as Zero Mostel; he has the look we all wear, except for a few chic hangers-on, the look of bare survivors, of a wreck that went under like a stone. We're surprising to ourselves; we don't know how we made it ashore; couldn't tell if asked. John is unacceptable in his field—ethics—to any Catholic university in the land, Jesuits included. I'm somewhat less immediately notorious. But the security, the credit cards, the sound ID went down in the catastrophe referred to above. Now we live by our wits, so to speak. (I forgot to ask John if the figure would fit him;

as for myself, a beneficiary of Cosmic Welfare, I live off the universe, an edgy method, never a dull moment.)

In the matter of John McNeil, I have pursued all available documents. I can only report they do not amount to much, qualitatively speaking. Letters from Rome, in this case as in the preceding centuries of decrying and decreeing, are not exactly *Star Wars* for scintillation or "Kojak" for bite. They are more like, gustatorially speaking, last week's omelette: cold but wholesome, with a cross cut into their flab to render them less indigestible. You realize why Rome never needs machines to turn out its letters; the mother church has ecclesiastic hacks who write as well, or as badly, as machines, but less expensively. Besides, what machines would give that nice, inhuman turn of a blade that has, so to speak, a cross on its hilt and therefore blesses even while it wounds—wounds against justice, against charity, against common sense, against reason itself?

The letters, to coin a cliché, run the gamut. The gamut is predictably narrow. One does not write from Rome, in the ordinary course of things, to express jubilation, or thanks for a work well done, or a poem turned, or a jail sentence survived; not for an exile rescinded, a Roman crime admitted and atoned. Such functions do not befit the functionary. No, in every case the message and the media are more purgatorial; they have the quality of fire to the touch. They urge repentance, submission, silence, withdrawal—the conduct generally befitting repentant children snatched by adult hands from lapse or lunacy.

This is somewhat the tone of the McNeil file. It should be added, in justice, that the hand of Father General Arrupe is generally not equal to his task. His humanity breaks through, in ways we have seen before, on happier occasions. One has a sense that he writes such letters with two-thirds or even half a heart, that in such matters as lie in contention here, he has been pushed to the wall and acts under duress. Uncommon courage, uncommon travail. In a good time, a good man may be both adroit and easefully large of spirit; but Arrupe's heroism is of a sterner cast, harder won. He lives in a time of leveling; he salvages what he can. He has, moreover, been nearly leveled himself on several occasions, living as he does under the gun sights of the Roman curia.

But to resume. Bizarre goings-on are transpiring, not isolated events, a crazy continuum, America, now. The Jesuit McNeil, on the threshold of distinction, an expert in ethics, a man well loved, held in respect—such a one begins speaking up on behalf of homosexuals. Not content with keeping closet matters where in decency they belong, and keeping such people where they belong, and urging on them contentment with their lunatic lot—no, he refuses that way, which is the time-honored way, the way the church has invariably gone, so that matters that belong in the light may stand in the light, and other unlovely, barely mentionable matters may dwell where fate (correction, God's will) assigns them: in the shadow. This Jesuit refuses to follow that way. He takes a few of these people by the hand and leads them into the very center of the circle—the circle, let us say, of worship, of brother and sisterhood. He introduces them to other Christians; he blesses them, shrives them, communicates them, just like the others. Everything is seemly and normal and aboveboard. In Christ, he says, there is neither hetero nor homo, but one Body, His own.

Now, this activity approaches the dangerous, and some people wince, and mutters of disaffection are heard. John seems not to hear them. If he does hear them, he grants them no attention. He is, as I suggested, one of Kierkegaard's *enfants terribles*, a "religious individual," out of tune, out of step. He has held a hand in his own, has sensed human suffering, has witnessed injustice, psychic destruction, stigma, rejection. From this gesture he takes the measure of the world, the measure of church teaching, the measure of his own soul. And so he walks one step further. It is not that he is ignorant, that he does not know he is on thin ice. Rather, he makes small account of such things; or at least (there is no point in creating a fiction here, a human without fear) he makes less account of personal danger than of the untended and unmerited suffering that his "prudence" would only worsen.

He takes a step. He does a classic thing, which Jesuits have done for centuries in such circumstances. He puts to work his skills and discipline and conscience. (The latter is the rub; he is not the typical bankrupt academic; he is incapable of the betrayal of silence.) He sets to work at a thorny, all but untouchable, urgent, human issue. In 1970, for *The Homiletic and Pastoral Review*, McNeil wrote three watershed articles entitled "The Christian Male Homosexual." The unsayable was said; the ghosts were out of the closet.

He was encouraged to expand on his ideas in a book. He did so and duly submitted the manuscript to the scrutiny of superiors. So far, simple. But what followed is probably one of the most extended eking-out of reluctant approbation in all the slow turning of Roman mills. In those months and years, I saw a new side of McNeil: the strength of absolutely marmoreal patience. To this day, I am trying to absorb and understand it. He waited, he questioned, he was rebuffed, he waited, once more he was told to wait, he was counseled to be patient by millenial-minded authorities. His manuscript was scrutinized by enough experts to sanitize the Augean stables. Their fine-tooth comb declared him again and again tick-free, lice-free, dandruff-free; gnat or camel, they could find nothing to stick at. Through it all he was unfailingly, exasperatingly courteous, a gentleman *ad unguem*. I watched and marveled and began to think the lapsarians wrong. Here was a Jesuit who escaped the lamentable common fate, when our garden became a spoiled playground. Where was his rancor, exasperation, his coil and recoil, the sweat and bruises we all bear into the public arena?

More, while he waited and waited for a Roman decision on his manuscript, McNeil's patience was an uncommonly active virtue. The organization Dignity, which he helped found for homosexual Catholics, grew to some fifty-six chapters in as many cities. And when his book was finally cleared and *The Church and the Homosexual* appeared bearing its croix de guerre, the imprimatur, McNeil took to the road like a shot. He visited some thirty cities speaking on behalf of gays, advancing the thesis of his new book:

> It would appear to follow that the same moral rules apply to homosexual as to heterosexual attitudes and behavior. Those

that are responsible, respectful, loving and truly promotive of the good of both parties are moral; those that are exploitive, irresponsible, disrespectful, or destructive of the true good of either party, must be judged immoral.

Which may be so, or may not. In any case, the bearing of a book or a baby into our world is, in the nature of things, a beginning of trials, misadventures, ogres, and angels. Not the end of these, by any means.

It appears that Rome was less than comforted by this successful delivery, a book that was born, loud and kicking in the world. We can only reconstruct events and motives here. On the one hand, the Congregation for Doctrine and Faith is not to be confused in method or ethos with the defunct crusher that preceded it, the Holy Office. Nor need we envision a lurking special interest, as though the Vatican had a corner on the construction of vertical coffins for uppity gays. The past suggests another direction. Simply, since the twelfth century, this unmanageable question of homosexuality has been managed quite well, through a tactic of queasy silence, eyebrow raising, public and private defamation, corporal punishment, auricular confession and forgiveness, the amendment of dark minds and darker acts. Let things stand at that, forever. Let such people be. Or in the inelegant but telling phrase of one Jesuit authority in this matter, "Kiss them off."

In any case, alternately kissed and kicked by fate, McNeil and his saga are far from ended. In August of 1979, John was summoned to New York Jesuit headquarters by Father Eamon Taylor, the provincial authority. He was informed that a letter from Father General Arrupe conveyed a decision of Cardinal Seper, head of the Roman Congregation of Doctrine and Faith. To wit: McNeil's book took a position contrary to the common teaching of the church; the book showed disrespect for the magisterium, appearing as it did just at the time the church had reaffirmed its position on the immorality of homosexuality; moreover, approval had been issued on the supposition that the book would be restricted to the community of scholars—but in consequence of McNeil's strenuous travels and many media appearances, Catholic gays were being deluded as to their true state.

In consequence of all this, the imprimatur was to be removed from future printings of the book, and McNeil was forbidden to speak henceforth on matters of sexuality or sexual ethics.

Roma locuta. Or so we heard. The Seper-Arrupe document was, as they say, "unavailable."

McNeil promptly and predictably obeyed, sending off a message to Chicago, where he was to address the opening session of the Dignity convention:

> . . . After a great deal of prayer and consultation I have personally made the decision to obey the directive. It was always my hope and dream that through my scholarship and efforts, I could make some contribution to a reconciliation of the church with the gay community, and of the gay community to the church. At this time and under these circumstances, I now judge that the best contribution I can make to that dream is by my silence. I hope by my silence to be of service both to the church which I love and the gay community with which I have become so closely identified.
>
> I hope also that my silence itself will be eloquent. I hope it will join the silence of those many theologians of pre–Vatican II, Teilhard de Chardin, John Courtney Murray, Henri de Lubac, whose obedience eventually led to their vindication. I would like my silence in some way to symbolize the defenseless silence through the centuries, and even today, of hundreds of thousands of gay Catholics. I am absolutely confident that this represents only a temporary setback in the cause of justice for gay Catholics and that, eventually, with God's help, the church will learn to deal openly and lovingly in dialogue with the gay community; that it will hear what the Holy Spirit has to say to the church from its gay brothers and sisters in Christ.

McNeil's response, whatever its merits, runs true to form. He refuses to play the loser or victim, to lie down on command and die. At the same time, he will not go away, thereby solving a dilemma that is not so much his as Rome's. Indeed the Great Leveler plays a sad charade in a sad time of disaffection and ill feeling—an atmosphere that church authority, in spite of all, seeds in the air. A "time of leveling": It demeans everyone, it stains everything.

We are indeed being leveled off. Kierkegaard's image is the

opposite of an order of things in which the proper dignity of all is respected, nurtured. Leveling: not creatureliness, nor a befitting modesty before the universe and God. Something other, indeed: a radical inversion of right order; dead principles invoked despite the cries of the living; women literally "put in their place" by a male blow; homosexuals eased into outer darkness, out of sight, out of mind. A closing of ranks, a closing of minds, a narrowing of the range of inquiry open to believers. And a warning served on others: on homosexuals who seek ordination or membership in religious orders—on all in fact, hetero, homo, or plain human, who hoped, had been led to hope, that the church was becoming an advocate of the victimized.

Alas, for the poor blokes that we are, and our dreams. We shall have to make our way as best we may in the mine fields, McNeil and many others, marginal to a church that itself is marginal to human hope. A marginal church, not in the Pauline sense of "unconformed to this world." To the contrary, a church all too conformed, all too powerful, all too fearful, all too prudent. That which should elevate and enhance—levels. That which should foster distinction, variety, passionate conscience—levels. That which should raise the dead, the equivalent dead, the presumed dead, the sentenced to death, the outcast, the victimized—levels. That which should confer faith and hope and charity, poisons us with bad faith, diminishes our hope to the vanishing point, comes toward us small and sour of mind.

But these reflections are meant to be an act of love. I am not sure I find McNeil's response to my crude taste. It is somewhat too mystical, it takes refuge, it is not angry. I hope he is not too resigned, just as I am sure he is not hateful. But apart from all that, I honor him. Today, when every conceivable question is politicized out of its reasonable skull, he places a sure, patient, obscure sense of soul above every crude feint or ploy. I suspect his sense of history is sound, and this not merely as a tactic. I think he is unafraid of the cross.

Storming some purported barricade might win him a feverish following; his silence brings us up short, leaves us perplexed, at sea. And at sea is where we are, in any case. It is bitter to be reminded of it: that we have few landmarks; that in this matter, as in so many others that have surfaced these past years, the church seems to have lost its bearings. Could the Roman officials have known that they have silenced McNeil at a most dangerous time, when homosexual rights are under fire and domestic fanatics are tuning up for a war on deviants? One wonders, one is appalled.

And what of the homosexual community? In New York, the archdiocese has consistently opposed an ordinance that would guarantee civil rights to gays. Gays have now been served notice, even as women previously were told by church officials, in terms silken or devious, that they are of no account, or of lesser account, or niggers, or irrelevant, or back-pew citizens, or unfit for ministry, or sexually unfortunate, or emotionally inferior, or . . . The degradation is wonderfully inventive; the intention is by now clear. Homosexuals will continue to be regarded in the church with that cute cast of the eye that signals more eloquently than a blow that a creepy citizen has somehow gotten into the compound. An emotional apparatus is then set in motion, somewhat as though a gorgeous dish were sailing past a knot of thugs on some midtown street. You can all but hear the gears revving up.

What should be seen in modest everyday terms, a meeting of humans, a celebration of variety, is sexualized, abnormalized. As in a scene played under water or in outer space, grotesque gestures, gyrations, come into play. We are shaken up, tumbled about, as though we were encountering freaks, the unmentionable (those who are showing us our own secrets, our throttled humanity?).

Then what? We hitch up our purported bumptious normalcy; we come on tougher than ever, more macho than ever. Whose church is this, anyway? Our church, male to the crotch, white to the real estate, pure to the very conception.

I feel like saying to John McNeil: Welcome aboard! After forty years, some twenty of them years of bare survival in the Jesuits, one feels entitled even to propound a principle—into the void, into the west wind. To wit: Every status in the American church

worth talking about, worth standing in, worth struggling for—
every one is under suspicion, threatened with wipeout.

And further, just about everything else is hogwash, captiva-
tion. I do not know why this is so; I am unhappy that it is so.
I sense that it was the Vietnam war that brought matters to this
pass. The war decade was a kind of judgment scene; old preten-
sions were utterly destroyed, old suppositions derided. The
official church went with the bloody tide, went down with it.
That church became an American invention, a tool of polity, a
blessing laid on unutterable violence. And the punishing fallout
fell not merely on the Vietnamese; it fell on us, broke us apart
like tinder. We staggered out of that decade scarred and broken.

Today we are acculturated to more and more violence, spent
as to spiritual energies, disoriented as to our direction, frivolous
or nostalgic as the whim takes us, ready for more degraded law
and order—to inflict it, to conform to it. A leveled church,
indeed, in a leveling time.

Kierkegaard implies it; how fond it would be in such a time,
for individuals cursed with a conscience, or determined on plain
speech, or laboring under galling maltreatment, or passionate
concerning the fate of others—how foolish for such to seek a
hearing. Their cause, their presence, their gifts are unwelcome.
They are not cogs. That is their sad destiny. And if they push
things, their destiny can become their crime. This is the alche-
my, the witch's brew that, once taken, levels us off. Homosexuals should be content with their crepuscular status; a dark target
is harder to hit. And there are worse outcomes: Other societies,
other times, have known how to deal with them, not in grudging
toleration, but condignly.

Thus, they (and we) take risks. Or we do not. We maintain a
certain minimal flame of spirit—or we do not. American society,
and the American church, will tolerate us as parasites, or peace-
niks, or good, abstract, paper-pushing academics, or hapless
citizens with grievances to be referred to Congress or polls or
votes or bread or circuses or confession or good works. Anything, that is to say, which gives solid evidence of moral limp-
ness. But to speak out, to act out, to translate good intentions
into sensible acts . . .

Many times in these years I have been placed in durance by the United States for standing at the Pentagon along with some friends, for declaring, however symbolically and mildly, that the destruction of the world by ever bigger and newer nukes seemed a not good idea. For dramatizing this unusual thought, I have been sentenced to jail. As we were rounded up on one occasion, I was able to slip from my wrists the plastic cuffs wherein I was held and conceal them on my person. Upon release, I sent this folkloric device as a gift to our Father General Arrupe, who was then celebrating his golden jubilee as a Jesuit. A straight-faced letter came back in due course, thanking me. The issue I had hoped to raise, the deadly and doughy silence of American Jesuits and American Christians with regard to the likely annihilation of all who walk the world, was of course not engaged. It is a time of leveling; one raises nothing, not the dead, not a few questions of life and death.

Dear Brother John McNeil, we shall have to content ourselves with perhaps two simple acts, which I take it are nearly all we can do today. First of all, we must continue to slip the chains and bonds from our hands (and feet and tongues and souls). This idea is too simple to need developing. We can go along with their silencing us; we can go along to their jails; but we must do these things with all our passionate hearts, for our good reasons, for our people, knowing our cause is just and worthy and speaks for all. We must not go in their direction hang-dog, like dogs to their own hanging. And second, we must offer strange gifts to authority. And the best gift I can think of is our own rebirth, our liberation. Something embarrassing, something sublime; come along that freedom road!

·7·

THE MOTHER

It occurred to me long after my mother's death (and perhaps the thought was salutary, removed from self-esteem or raw grief) that such a woman might safely have been entrusted with the fate of the world.

Can this be considered sensible, a reflection whose danger is drawn like the sting of a nettle, by long grief subsided?

Let me say it. She could be entrusted with the world. She was providential, foreseeing, compassionate, a woman who without self-aggrandizement had a weather eye out for virtually all weathers. And modest; she had no great interest in her own repute or stature, the difference her life might be thought to make. Knowing her place in a scheme of things; a place larger, not smaller, than she knew.

Six children, boys. A husband. Take from her all modern conveniences, devices, accouterments. Except in late middle age, when she, like any modern woman, could turn a switch and her hard work was relieved.

Before that, it was labor and labor—in more senses than one. The labor of bringing children into the world. Each, we learned, had been a wrenching agony. And each child, once born, made another mouth at table, another to clothe and house and nurse and love and worry over. Each different, each calling into play ingenuity, wisdom, a different language, to persuade, cajole, urge into self-sustaining humanity, pride. "The way we live, or try to live, is the way you're invited into. Come along."

Philip and I were the two youngest. If her body had given up, if she had said in the teeth and glare of the family and their priest and nun, "I've had it," then of course we would not be here—to tell, to raise hell. Thank you.

Take away her work, take away her house, her garden, the wash-day steam and chaos, the stove to be poked into a flare—like stripping a rich ear of corn, intent only on the husks.

This describes her extreme old age. But not the great early and middle years, when she literally created a future for so many.

Yet we never thought of her as extraordinary or spiritually gifted. Such simply did not enter into the equation of childhood. One had parents; the parents were good, bad or indifferent.

In our neighborhood, we had quite a spectrum: portents, horrors, smilers, punishers, softies, gorgons, everything. It didn't occur to ask, to remark, "Isn't our mother really something!" Or taking measure from some other, "Look at Ms. Sonso, she sure isn't up to momma." Though it could be said justly, turning 360 degrees in our neighborhood, any Ms. Sonso you could mention sure as hell wasn't.

The judgments of children are primitive, cruel, and allowing for wooden and puddin' heads and much selfishness (or self-interest), are strangely right. Or so it seems to me.

If I can put on a six- or ten-year-old head once more and look on that farm of ours—what homesickness, loathing, longing wells up! A deep vein is set pulsing, like a tube that branches out to nurture the body.

I find myself there once more; child of a landscape I open, like a hinged album drawn from some secret place.

I see the gray weather-scoured house, already old in my child-hood, set on its meager hillside, windows grudging and narrow like eyes sizing up their world, disliking what they see, morning to night. The barn leans on its haunches like a tired beast. Outhouse and chicken house out back, to the east the orchard where we buried old Maj (senile, dragging his neck to doom, the nag stood in his shallow grave and the boom! of the bullet sprayed his dim brains on the sod and clay). Beyond, eastward, fields stretched, nine or ten acres of corn and potatoes and berries, the kitchen garden south of the house beyond two wormy pear trees.

My mother, her gaze hemmed in by those windows. My mother's life, hemmed in by that house. A damp, floorless cellar underfoot, a cold set of bedrooms overhead. And on the third floor, an unfinished attic, three tiny windows, not so much offering light or cheer as spreading thick shadows meagerly. And above that thankless dungeon, like a cap on a dunce, a cupola; reached by a stair like the stair to a scaffold. Those two top enclosures smelling of dead bats and trapped birds. Eerily, once or twice in my boyhood, a bat or bird crossed my eyes in the perpetual dusk, terror on terror.

My mother's house. That inert, comfortless dwelling, which custom, religion, ceremony, the imposed myth that is crueler by far than plain fact—all these would conspire to insist: This is a home. My mother was, so to speak, no nominalist. My father was. This is one way of putting the hurt, the conflict. When my mother was absent, the "home" froze in its bones. It went rigid; it became a house of blocked ice, of will, of myth. A former home. Which is to say, a house.

A house that my father, aided and abetted at all times by his chorus of sisters (those nominalist fates and furies), insisted on calling a home. "Home!" they would exclaim. "You boys must be grateful for so good a home!" They did protest too much. And we sat there and endured, or disappeared from sight and endured. Awaiting her return.

For your absence was, to a small boy, the hugest hole in the universe. When you went to town, disappearing down the road in the old teetering streetcar, the boy turned disconsolately indoors, closed the door, strove with his small brother to be brave and good, to wash a few dishes and sweep a floor. Then the home dropped its jaw and stopped breathing. You were not there. It made little difference that you were less than three miles distant, that you would return before sundown. What difference did such mitigations make, against what were time and distance measured (three hours, three miles)? They belonged properly to those twice one's size and thrice his years! They did not signify, any more than if one were told, "Your mother is dead, but be comforted, sweet bye and bye, on that beautiful shore . . ." Such wrong strokes, such dumping of straw in the void! It falls, falls in a dead well of loss.

She was gone from the house, she was gone from the world. With no exaggeration, this is what I remember. If the father came in from work and she had not yet returned, his presence added nothing of recourse or consolation. Indeed, because he was feared and she was loved and lacked, his coming made one want to flee for dear life. A voice whispered, "She is gone." Then it added, "Flee." It was sound advice, and the boy obeyed.

I look back on that child (yet I do not look back, he is here before me). He is studious and owlish, goes by a nickname both contemptuous and affectionate—"Four Eyes." He is known to disappear for hours, crouching in some out-of-the-way corner, wrapt in a book.

Not to be deceived. It is a ploy, his way of keeping out of sight, buried as his spirit is in a more or less constant wretchedness. Behind a book, the boy is out of ear and eyeshot of the father, that anger against a nonconforming, maladroit specimen.

My father lived through fifty-four years of marriage, handsome and complete in frame, an exiled Irish king among yahoos. So he saw himself.

A question arises: How did I see him?

A missing part; a hole perhaps in the heart, or a hole where a heart should have been. An essential lack; something that could not be "cosmetically corrected."

Yet it must be understood that he was neither a drunkard nor a common brute, nor was he unfaithful in the strict sense. To his credit must be set down, in all fairness, his hard, bruising labor, a near religion of labor, the most un-Catholic ethic in this matter; self-punishment, ineptitude for repose. Settle in a comfortable chair? He shrank from comfort as from a bed of nails or coals. Thus even his love of work, if it could be called that, turned sour, turned against others. Uneaseful tension sprang from his frame like an emanating leap, a reproach to the longed-for repose of my mother. He kept things on edge; his presence was like the whirr of an emory wheel on a blade—it set off sparks.

He loved good talk; but it had to turn on his topic, pursued at his sweet will. The method veered about; now it was a snarled ball of monologue, again a kind of Socratic bark and bite. You kept trying to follow the yarn (literally), to unknot, disengage. You showed the best will in the world. After all, this wayward game was preferable to his other one, an appalling icy silence. . . . After which you were brought up short as he barked out a question meant, one presumed, to engage your wits, to bring light on some matter or other.

In my case, it did exactly the opposite. It was as though he seized a length of the yarn and effectively tied up my tongue. I remember to the hour one of those barks, gone off like a firecracker in the face. I was reduced on the spot to a mute for some fifteen minutes, at the end of which period, evidently convinced that nothing further was to be expected from the dummkopf, he resumed his yarn snarling.

Had there been two such parents instead of one, had my mother been cursed with the temperament of any one of his sisters, then it would have been all up with the six sons. In the tundra of upper Appalachian clay that surrounded us, an unpromising, poverty-ridden waste of isolation, bitter winters, and often fruitless summers, there dwelt families driven insane by such parents, in tandem working their worst on one another and on their hapless children.

We were saved from that. Whatever substance has accrued to our lives, whatever goodness, must be laid at our mother's feet. Tardily, with an aching sense of the lateness of the gift and of her loss, I lay it there.

He worked like a demon for years and years, at a series of humiliating, paltry jobs that could have been filled by a lout.

His religious life requires a word, as does hers.

My mother's was a practical German piety, unselfconscious, a matter of yea and nay, intellectual only in the sense of being firmly held and consequential. She knew what she believed; she saw no reason either to parade her belief abroad or to inflate its scope. The "day of worship" brought in its wake no contrary or competing rhythm; only an enlarged, refined, slowed sense of her life. Sunday descended on her like a shekinah; she arrayed herself in her poor best; she appeared with a hardly won majesty before the Lord.

And her family too; they were summoned on Sunday to their best conduct and costume, for thus was it written.

We became, over the years, whether in the old Model T Ford or the streetcar or bus, or on foot, or hitchhiking, or in the later grandeur of an Olds—we became the indefatigable, the redoubtable, the church-goers supreme; a family whose arrival in the Holies the Almighty might have set the clocks of the universe by, with a nod of satisfaction and a slight adjustment of the mighty stem of things.

However. The sabbatarian rest by no means appealed to my father. A command to slow down? A far different voice sounded in my father's bones, twitched him like a goad. Often as not after mass, in summer, he beckoned to himself spirits more restless than he, ordered one or several of the sons out of doors with him, in prospect of something offhandedly announced as a "look around the place." Which cursory look, soon dispensed with, was followed oftener than not, by the appearance, as though conjured out of thin air, of tools of trade, hammers, saws; and then, of stooped bodies over the furrows, above the workbench. "A plain scandal to the neighbors," my mother would cry. All in vain.

Religious matters could be summed up in the simple, unchanging quality of a face. Which is to say, my mother took on no special "Sunday look." If at mass she seemed remote, even wrapt, still the cast and coherence of her features were intact. When she turned from prayer to attend the rambunctious child at her side, and gravely shook her head in disapproval, and turned back to the altar, there was a sweetness and suavity, even an elegance in the gesture. It impressed itself, that turn of the beautiful head from profile to full face and back. The universe was attending to me. The motion met the soft wax of the child's mind; the wax was cast in the metal we name memory; it rests there to this day.

The sixty-year-old public man consults the child, that owlish undersized one, big glasses tilted on his button nose—and he finds no clue.

The man ponders, consults himself. Mother and father are long dead, the argument of these pages perhaps better buried with them. But he cannot bury it. Pressing, haunting as the question of unknown parentage, is the question of his mother's survival, her clues, coloration, the springs of her soul; these cling to him. He would rather be mistaken than be ignorant. He senses that in reaching longingly toward her ghost as she recedes on time's waters—in that gesture, though a mess of shadows mock his tears; still the effort strangely suffices. He touches her; if he merely touches the hem of her garment, the odor of memory.

She was lonely, lonely. But so, I reflect, were most country wives; with the added sting, in her case, that she refused the common devices that bonded country women: card playing and gossip.

Lonely. I write the word and write it again. The word is forged in the ice and fire of maturity. We children were never, as I recall, lonely. That corrosion began later, under rejection and contumely.

I do not want to dramatize her plight, an injustice to the sweetness of spirit she fought for, in the teeth of the world, and finally attained. She was no stoic; she had no armor against the world. She was supple, free, a contemplative, an inward-looking spirit. This was her secret, and her salvation.

Granted, she was out of her element, in furious seas; granted, the skiff was unseaworthy. Once she had pushed off from shore and the voyage formally blessed, a course set; if things went awry and ruin impended—what then was she to do? Was she perhaps to step out of the boat and walk on waters?

There is no untangling things, except in memory, that fusing force and healer.

There was no untangling things, when life was knotting and tightening, and in every way open to perversity and ill luck, going wrong. It was only to be borne; a passive role in grammar but, in reality, a life that, like impeded streams, found its own way—around, under.

She is by far the more difficult of the two to conjure up. My father is fifteen years dead, but his ghost still stalks us—his sardonic, inspired, Irish-Yankee lingo, his wit and witlessness, the moods that made us cringe. He pushes into the mind, jostles for a place there.

Her ghost lies still, or sits, or moves about, always quietly, claiming no attention: a great listener, one whose life is a moving light. Her face is averted; she is like a Strindbergian emanation; her face is veiled from us.

She sits at a kitchen table in winter, reading; always alone. And if she is interrupted by an importunate child, she may suddenly erupt in wild despair, "Leave me alone, leave me alone!" (The day has been too much, the years too much . . .)

Why recall such things, her tears, we standing there dumb and helpless?

In memory there is healing.

No private faces in public places. All photos of the family, including the fresh-faced, dog-collared clerics, were placed in rooms off bounds to any but the immediate family.

This was a strict rule of hers. The family was one thing, friends and acquaintances another. There was no mixing the two; of that would come only confusion of mind and divided loyalties and frivolous pride. Her house was not an inn, nor was her mind. On such matters she never yielded.

The elemental things of the world exclude tragedy and comedy. Water and fire know nothing of conflict, desire; they go their own way. And when we borrow these elements for the sake of human analogy, we enter a kind of Zen world, in which simplicities are restored; as though we too, rendered perfect as water and fire, were "beyond" anguish and farce.

These elements of creation make no history; at least in the Western sense, where history is inevitably the record of ruthless winners, warriors and liars, duplicitous diplomats, bloodshot juntas and shahs and their clerical clones; leveling adversaries, creating lost peoples, slaves, and victims.

My father was voracious after a name, a history. He sought fame as a shark scents its meat. But fame is more than a prey; something he never learned. Not idly the ancients called fame a woman; in the subtle arts and arena of courting and enticing and winning love—in this he was no subtler than a shark, shooting toward its prey. Alas, for him, he hungered and hunted in vain.

My mother made no history; women commonly make no history. Is it because they have other, less sharklike appetites?

She was very like the woman at the well whom Jesus encountered. For a short time, this woman made a little noise, a small tumult. She was the occasion of his committing a scandal; he, a rabbi, attentive to her, a woman and a Samaritan, double indemnity.

And this is very nearly all we know of her. She ran to tell her village about the strange man of the mountain who, in her crude phrase, "told me all I had done." In her eyes, he seemed a kind of Magian, a necromancer; but strangely merciful too, beyond her experience of men (which, we are informed, was considerable).

The townsfolk came running, half in bored excitement, half in good-natured contempt for "her type." This is the last we hear of her, a woman who occasioned one of the deepest epiphanies of the Fourth Gospel. She is nameless. Can one imagine a male occasioning so long and important a discourse of the Lord—and remaining nameless? She does a very great thing and disappears into it.

A nun said to me, discussing this passage, "She's like all of us. What do we count for?"

It is important for me to ponder why this is so, why women are of less account. But also this: What is the countering strength, the countervailing truth? On the one hand, the "apostles," "disciples," "friends" are given a name, a history, an exalted, specific task in the world; while the women are left shadowy, anonymous, mere messengers, intermediaries.

In my mother's life, commonly esteemed things like money, ego, a mighty fortress of a God, a bloodletting bloodline—these were forbidden, taboo. They could not confer beatitude, in this world or any other. She went another way. And God, who is commonly merciless to the merciful, tested her fiercely. Her life became a desert. And living that life, which is the common life and calling of Christians, she became what she was called to: a resplendent ikon of that *aurea media* praised by the ancients, Christians and others.

There could have been, God knows, a better marriage; there could also have been less contentious, clamorous offspring.

Her life could have been less dreadful, less routine-ridden and work-ridden—and her life would, by modern standards, still qualify as moderately awful.

All this is true, according to modern measure. And yet I

remember also, for this is the chief point of her story, its commendation—her life struck others as a gentle, a rhythm of peace and spiritual plenty.

Talk about an achievement!

Her life: comedy, tragedy, farce, tragicomical farce. It was all there, the meld and mix of our condition. And it was written and choreographed (and largely staged) by my father.

Her face changed. It was not merely that she grew older. She bore too much; she grew ashen, weary, a look of bare endurance appeared.

They were married in a little country church in northern Minnesota, by a priest whose sepia photo, dignified and old-fashioned, hangs on my wall. He sits there, his long beard and broadcloth coat and big clerical book in hand; an impassive yet tender face, a look of sacrifice in the patriarchal eyes. And then two great, outsize hands: the left easeful and horizontal, holding his book erect on its spine; the other downward-pointing, resting on the chair arm. An Abraham at peace, a Moses on watch.

This priest has fame and holy repute among the Catholics of that region, having lived for many years the harsh life of the plains Indians, dwelt in their bark cabins in scorching and icy weathers, talked their language, eaten their food. His life is published; among many he is considered a saint. His bishop honored him in old age as "one of the two or three greatest missioners to have come to our shores." And by all evidence, deservedly.

In my boyhood, the picture of this priest was in our home for as long as I can recall. Was it an unconscious irony of the fates that his face should be the guardian saint of that union, blessed in the beginning by his laborer's hands; that the blessing should have brought us in the next generation—to this? Prison, the courts, near expulsion from my order, public contention, honor, dishonor? Surely he reached deep in the well of history, of early Christians, of the heart of Christ, to dredge up such a blessing.

We were the only family I knew, before or since, who in the course of some twenty years had no event in our midst to celebrate or mourn. No birth, death, marriage; no funeral or baptism. We traveled hardly at all, once we had made the west-east trek from Minnesota to New York State and dug in. Only one of us ever saw a stage play in New York. Our exposure to the great world was, in sum, roughly that of the Appalachian poor: few wants aroused, fewer satisfied. Our father saw us as he saw himself: workhorses, in harness or out.

Out of harness, the pleasures were mitigated, spartan. A movie was a rare delight; we hardly ever ate out, even in the most modest emporia.

This was an interesting anomaly. We were poor; we dwelt in a wide circuit of families in like plight or worse. We were poor, and for years we did not even know it. There were, in fact, few if any ways to test those words: *poor, nonpoor.*

I suppose we were simply part of what came to be known later as the "culture of poverty." Stuck in it, among the stuck. Such a conclusion a learned study would undoubtedly have come up with.

And yet I have little memory of unhappiness. That circle of ours, tightly drawn as it was, and stifling perhaps, inductive of a kind of naiveté, also had its compensations: We grew up as something more than appetites on the hoof. You had a few nickels in your pocket; more often than not, you had nothing. But the pockets of your brothers and your friends up and down the country road were similarly unburdened. So the coins made no great difference; what you had you were taught to share; there was little envy in the air.

Then, time passing, we started trekking to the parochial school, some two miles distant from home. There, a few yardsticks stood up, to take our measure. The country mice met the city mice; and here and there a son of the new rich or the near rich bumped or shouldered us out of the way. Thus we were instructed in their inalienable right to the right of way. Few specimens in the world are more arrogant, we learned, than the younger mandarins cast, for a time only (before Notre Dame or the College of New Rochelle), among swine and swineherds.

One winter night, my mother was grouped with three of the younger children in the kitchen. It was bedtime; she was about to shepherd us up the dark back stairs to the attic room. Bitter, that upstate cold that had the grip of a wolf upon a frozen shank.

She, who was normally uncomplaining and resilient of spirit, turned toward someone in the family (I do not know how the subject got broached). She said something that, all at once, in a tone I recall to this day, revealed the scalding grief that dwelt behind her eyes, her lonely gambit in the ugly, barren house, children to be fed and clothed and somehow kept alive and kicking. (And himself grandiose, above these petty concerns, wrapped in his ego.)

Exactly what she said I cannot recall, but I read her sense as though I were reading this moment the lips of her mind, or had heard her speak once more among the speechless dead. Something about the bitterness of poverty; what it cost, the bread and beans and macaroni and meat loaf. As though these must be dredged up from the center of the earth, dragged by main might across a continent, doled out, portion by portion, day after day, against odds beyond measure. This is the sense I keep: the burden of it, the dead weight of a poverty that was inexorable.

She turned and beckoned and we followed her up the stairs.

She grew ill.

There was something obscurely shameful about it, a contagion referred to ambiguously as a "spot on the lung." She was taken off to St. Joseph's Hospital (it was there, some fifty years later, the FBI were aided and abetted in their pursuit of me and their shadowing of her by the nuns in charge).

On Sundays, we three youngest were brought in to her bedside for a viewing. My father would trumpet our arrival: prize exhibits of his and the aunts' buffeting care. And my mother, pallid, gray as the linen of the bed, broke down in weak tears at sight of us; so skinny and underfed we were, she mourned later.

And came home from hospital before her cure was accomplished, to be ensconced in a bed just off the kitchen, so she could direct the older boys at cooking operations. "To get rid of his sister, that hellcat," she said with satisfaction, "to get her out of my house."

Back on her feet, she would board a senile streetcar, an hour's voyage each Monday, to mend clothing at an orphanage. There she gained a circle of friends, women her age or older. It cost next to nothing, and it extricated her for a space from the blank box of her life. And, oh, how it was resented, this mild excursion.

Like Mother Courage, willy-nilly, knowing that she could neither make wars nor unmake them, she dragged her cart through the hideous carnage of the century. All those wars, which finally are one war!

Unlike Mother Courage, she had neither the wit nor the flamboyant, easy conscience to make a buck where she could, to con victors or victims. Neither did her religion come wrapped in a flag. I see her as a kind of holy drudge, never quite broken; her gifts pressed hard, ground under; the lost chance, the bad luck she put on with her wedding ring, the sacrament: thou shalt, thou shalt not. And there she must stand: outside the circle she could not take a stand. It had been taken for her. Truly, possibility had been taken from her.

But not all. To hem her in too closely is to do her injustice, just as to "make her an example of Christian womanhood, etc." is to do her an injustice.

Let me do her justice, take the measure of that circle in which she must live and grow old and die. And in which, covertly, and without an ear to attend to her, she may yet dream.

She sent four sons off to World War II, that virtuous, blood-sodden threshing floor. Four sons to war, a fifth incapacitated, myself in seminary. She hung the four stars in the window; most days, my father put out a flag. The house, with only the two of them, was vacant as a ghost's eyes, shadowy with voices and memories.

Comely is a word that occurs.

This is a boy's inarticulate awe of his mother. His life is raw and incomplete. He must look upward, see what the world and time make of that other, that improbable friend and mentor.

She was comely. I choose the old-fashioned word with care. It bespeaks an aura, a worldly style and verve, tart opinions, a mind of her own.

And otherworldly too, a woman of devotion.

A scene sticks in the boy's mind. In the cold northern bedroom of the house stood a portent of note, a five-foot statue of the Blessed Virgin. It had been deposited with us on the basis of some vague loan ("until required") by a local convent of nuns.

My mother, who abominated all display, including the religious pavane of the Irish, commonly made her devotions before this image. But only after the boys had been dispatched to school, and my father departed for work.

The memory of her, kneeling on the floor, in the winter cold, her shoulders draped in an ugly, maroon shawl—the memory is a grace, a mere accident (the boy at home ill, wandering into the room where she knelt).

The boy knew nothing of beauty, conventional or otherwise. People around were as alike as a bundle of sticks: short, fat, tall, sticks with faces. He knew, however, something about function, conduct, rhythm, holding and withholding. And what he saw in his mother, what he understood without a word to back him up, or the need of a word, was an effortless (he thought it effortless) overflow of soul, brimming over the body like water over a limestone sheer; forming as it flowed. Hers was something of that "too much" that makes of the normal and good too little. This is why, to the boy, other women, mothers of his friends, paled before her.

Hers was the beauty of imbalance, dissonance, the soul that overflows, all but overwhelms.

This is a strange thing, that the soul should be so in command: "A terrible beauty is born." Captive, reconciled; but unreconciled too, and free.

There was a Christmas ritual.

A skinny tree, a few lights and trinkets, a gift or two. To the boy, what a miracle!

On that morning a great to-do arose surrounding small matters. Dining plates had been set out the night before, around the living-room table, a name beside each place. Sometime during the night, the mother, helped by one of the older boys, placed on each plate, meagerly or generously, depending on the current state of the exchequer, the following items: a handful or two of hard candy, three or four chocolates, an orange. Beside, a toy or an article of new clothing.

A clamor arose on Christmas morning at sight of such wonders! (No containing oneself; nor, indeed, any effort worth speaking of to contain us.) Our own portion, slice, the edible, delightful world! The boy enchanted, astray in his wits; why, the world itself was made of rock candy! See, a morsel of that world falls to his hands!

The round plate from which he has eaten, day after dull day, his dull portion; now a few trifles are heaped on it: colors, smells, the very marrow of happiness!

The world cheats, ever-larger portions, stakes, enterprises, Pyrrhic conquests. Other Christmases, better gifts, we weigh what lies in our hands; our eyes take on the narrowed meanness of those who know a pennyweight of gold from a pound of feathers. And all is lost.

One Christmas there arose a bustle and hurry like that of all previous Christmases. An older boy was awakening the others: Hurry! What gifts, what wonders lay in store . . .

We knew, we did not know. Tactile, sweet-smelling Christmas awaited.

Then the mother appeared in the doorway. She wore a different face, a grave and steady and searching look. Not her Christmas face by any means; a suffusion of sweetness unfeigned and warnings only half-purposed.

She shook her head sorrowfully. What could this mean?

Children, she murmured, this year there are no gifts. We have no money for gifts. I want you to be grateful instead for what we have—a good Christmas dinner.

Too poor that year. No Christmas extras. Gratitude, a good dinner. The statement was bare bones, the bones of things laid bare (where, to be sure, there had been no great accretion of fat).

Indeed, the world was no rollicking, big-bellied Santa, giving out with his phony haha of beatitude. So fetid a myth had never been invoked in our family, on Christmas or during the lean years. More, the children had witnessed, as a very law and procession of time, the long, dolorous line of poor and homeless and hungry men knocking at the door of our farmhouse, lurching figures set in motion by the world's engine, telling the time unbearably close, the tolling of truth itself. This is the way the world goes! This is the way! Thus it is ordained! Thus ordained!

There was sobriety in the dovecote that morning, but no long faces, no noses out of joint. The world was not made of rock candy, not even for an hour, one morning of the year. The world was made, if eyes were lucid and unafraid, of adamant; and those who struck against it were battered, and many died.

Christmas morning. It might be that a reluctant door of stone would open, ecstatic messengers issue from a dark cave, bearing gifts. This might or might not occur. That it usually had occurred by no means established a law or an obligation. The laws incised on stone did not include compassion or generosity. The laws were rather those of gravity (everything at length falls, the rule of death) and the law of the stars (we're deaf, don't shout so).

My mother knew the charm, the open sesame that unlocked the door of Ironbound Mountain. She knew it by heart and pronounced it distinctly; but the mountain did not invariably budge. And thereby we learned, eventually, yet another lesson. In the mountain lurked no magic at all, but a Master and Mountebank, who in mischief or testing or cruelty or caprice (we never knew) might deign to open the door. Or might not.

Did my mother know, on the morning in question, what impelled the *Magister Ludi* to play deaf and dumb? I think she knew no more than we, and I think she knew infinitely more than we. She trusted; that was all.

She had little to say about the early years of her marriage, especially as those years touched on my father. I suspect it was in reaction to the Irish, their keening for the "good old days." In any case, the past was a closed book whose text might, in accord with scripture, be sweet on the tongue; but it was also bitter as gall in the guts.

She lived too long not to be glad at times that most of living was over. Now and again, rarely, the boy was granted a glimpse of her young years; how sorrow and loss had lodged themselves, gross grains or fine, in the tissue of her life.

We loved to twit her, a mild form of harassment. Would inquire, in mock astonishment, "How did you ever come to marry *him?*"

Once (he still alive), she drew herself erect like a myna bird confronted with an offensive odor: "I'll have you boys know your father was considered a *great catch!*"

Again, in her old age, and he having departed this vale, we dared put the same question, malice aforethought. She turned away, paused for a long time. Then she turned on us, that candid, devastingly direct look: "You know, someone should have knocked me in the head!"

Depression years, and the drought. At the bottom of the heap (where our family dwelt, our appointed place in nature), whatever goes wrong hits hardest. I believe I have referred to us as northern Appalachian poor. My father, kicked out of his job, was taken on finally by one of the Works Projects Administration crews in the neighborhood. They set about creating a park on the shores of Onondaga Lake, including a salt-spring swimming pool.

We were at the bottom of the economic heap, but the bottom was made of good earth. We raised our own food, and enough to spare: an austere regime, but never a stingy one. With, often as not, one, two, or three strangers included at table.

And there was the famous three-wheeled cart. It became as near a part of Clay Farm existence as, on a loftier sabbatarian plane, did the galloping Model T, the latter strictly reserved, so to speak, for formal wear and tear.

But that cart! The aforementioned Mother Courage pushed or hauled about the stage of the world no more adaptable, high-spirited, splay-backed instrument of basic economy and appropriate technology and etcetera!

Consider its burdens and glories over those years. Fresh strawberries and Colombia berries and tomatoes, hawked with varying success in the neighborhood. Or, with a small, adjustable, lightweight rack placed on this excellent wooden nag, a round load of golden hay would arise, bumping from meadow to barn. Or a stash of shucked corn ears. Or on return voyages from here, there, anywhere, the two side wheels careening along at the bidding of hands at the crossbar: Behold our cart, liberated in spirit and fact, no longer a mere, mangy, woebegone beast of the poor. Now, more in the nature of a circus car or a rodeo bronco, possessing the tar road, hill and dale, motor traffic seldom intruding; the burden of the transmogrified cart being now simply—a boy! A starry-eyed, windy-haired, uneasy rider. He clung to the wooden flanks for dear life; he sat there like the Buddha in an earthquake. The more his vehicle shook him, wildly testing his faith in the God of the crossroads, why, the more loudly he flung abroad his laughing challenge to the shaman of storms. A laughing Buddha!

But the foregoing is no more than the economics of the red pushcart, the ecstatic progress of the cart, the celebratory bacchic cart.

There was quite another side to this mobile marvel. Therefore it shall be referred to hereafter as the Cart of Compassion. And it is at this point that the mother enters the scene, her spirit possessing, animating, revving up this remarkable chameleon chariot.

During those years of my childhood (as is far more terribly and universally true at present), food was a bitter question for many. Survival. The less-than-likely next meal. Surrounding us in the neighborhood were families for whom the cornucopia had dried up (the drought), or to whom it turned only its small, sealed, hind end (the depression). There were the ashamed poor, the aged poor, the shiftless poor, the unemployed and incapacitated and zonked, the country characters and ne'er-do-wells.

On these the skies, habitually beetling and overbearing, had quite brutally fallen. In little, tacky houses and hovels, off the main roads, in unnamed dead-end cinder paths where no cars ventured, among a few chickens and weeds and a dog and a rusty auto cadaver or two, dwelt such families or solitaries, eking out an unutterably miserable existence—the man- and God-forsaken country poor. Snot-nosed, bony kids, blank-eyed women, a nameless, ignored grandmother in some dank corner, the slack-shouldered, defeated men.

There were horrors, too, in those shanties and sheds: madness, violent spasms, wife beatings, murder, the raw ache and agony simmering in August heat, crouching indoors through the battering winters.

This is where the famous cart rolled in. Where this endlessly adaptive creature transmogrified once more. It became a kind of food bank on the move, a celebration of that promised land where all would be free and easy and the mystical goose hang high.

With regularity, we boys were dispatched by twos, to deliver free provender from the cart. To wit: in all seasons, tin pails or half-gallon bottles of fresh milk. And in season, all sorts and varieties of fresh produce from the garden: corn, spinach, potatoes, carrots, beans, berries; also apples, plums, prunes from the orchard. Also dairy products: fresh butter and cottage cheeses. These severally to Ms. Zapp and Ms. McDermott, who were bed-ridden; to the Bodys, who were purse-proud and brought low; to the Smiths, the most colorful and outrageous of all the colony of the lost; to Mamie and Oliver Powell and their snarling shepherd bitch (to Oliver because he was old as a fence post, a Civil War veteran; and to Mamie simply because she was mad and mean-spirited and terrorized the neighbors in fervent pursuit of both destinies).

Thus, my mother's largesse, which extended and widened the domestic table, was not exhausted at our board. How wickedly comparative a thing it is, I reflect, this little or much; how those scales marked "more" and "less" teeter madly in the chaos of America!

We scraped the unpromising land, and with a few domestic animals and labor that included all, we made it through some of the leanest years since Pharaoh turned out his seams.

My mother. She threaded many through the gospel's needle eye: ourselves and others. Convinced as she apparently was that others than the family must be gotten through such times; that, indeed, unless those others made it also, our own passage would be much impeded or summarily halted.

An example. Through her urging, there sat at our table frequently, among many others, a misfortunate clan whom I take even today as emblem of the abused human lot. The mother was a sour exile from obscure grandeur and mysterious wealth frequently invoked, with nose aloft and the wobbly eye of the born martyr. Her marriage, by her oft-rehearsed account, had brought her low. The guilty husband, paying in her uxorious swath for the sin of daring to exist, looked habitually bewildered and defeated, as though the fates had, at her hands, delivered him a blow intended for an ox. A truck driver, he had an even worse fate in store than his marriage.

One awful day, his vehicle killed a child in the streets, by account of witnesses, through no fault of his. And in mad shock or remorse, seeing the child fall under the wheels, he abandoned the truck and disappeared for months into the nearby swamps.

Ill luck multiplied and compounded. A baby had fallen from their second-story window, hovered for months between this world and a better. An older offspring, in concert with two other drifters, undertook to rob a country bank; and in the process, inept and edgy at their first heist, they shot and killed an old bank clerk who had not leapt to obey them quickly enough. The employee, it transpired, was stone deaf. The three gained not a cent and were captured in hours.

Ill luck, the bottom, the law, ill fortune kneaded grittily into the very dough of creation. Such families as these sat at our table or received food at their own door. The women among them stopped for hours at our kitchen, reciting their litanies of malice and woe. At our house, their children were counseled, reprimanded, praised—and fed. Talk about extended family!

Our family was lacking almost genetically in what is vulgarly known as American smarts. It was not that, from some Olympian motive, we disapproved of the theory and practice of the Great Upward Scramble. (I remember devouring the nincompoop novels of Horatio Alger, junk food for the mind, and finding, to say the least, nothing morally repulsive in those propulsive creations of low wit, flummery, and swerve.)

We were afflicted, so to speak, with the bad luck that saves, innocent as bumpkins in Shylock's clutches. We had no idea of what makes cash registers sing, what makes families get on top and stay there.

There were, in my father's background, any number of Irish who had gone from tidy little farms nearby, amassing their tidy little sack, to become petit bourgeois merchants in the city—of coal and ice, of hardware and dry goods and groceries. He rehearsed such wonders by the hour.

We used to speculate on this: why he never got anywhere in any of the numerous areas where his luck or skills might be applied. He worked the railroad, the assembly line, the steel mills, the power company. He was also an experienced farmer, mechanic, plumber; in his old age, he constructed a table for a Jesuit chapel. It was a piece of cunning, a wonder.

Then there was the writing: poetry, prose, reminiscences, humor, reams and reams, most of it written out in his hieroglyphic longhand—practically all of it worthless. But he kept it coming, like the great salt machine at the bottom of the sea.

My parents lived in a war-ridden world. They died, and nothing eased in the world.

Were they to return, they would find nothing eased in the world. War is still the universal coin; many are beggared; a few grow rich. There is less of the earth for most; there is war and threat of war and preparation for war and waste and rapine in service to war. The mad momentum gains ground every hour.

Only now, war would be claiming their grandsons instead of their sons.

They and we are thus caught in a warp of the unnatural. It leaves us with desperately narrowed choices, as it did them. To go with the horror named war; or to resist.

But either choice is, in a sense, unnatural. Silence is complicity, resistance is the task, perpetually repeated and set at naught, of Sisyphus the absurd.

This is a bitterness beyond telling. My parents bore us into a cultural and political and moral compact as to means and end. The compact was proclaimed as binding on all. Yet we spend our lives resisting the violation by highly placed authority (men beyond accountability or recourse) of that same compact.

My father died in 1969. My mother lived on for another decade, grew older in the cross fire of war. Through her whole life, up to (but not including) the Vietnam war, she had no instructor, no moral map. On this question of war, the first question of all, the question in comparison with which all others pale—on this question she, who was devout as a Teresa or Joan, had not even a church. She was simply one with the millions who perished, the millions who begat sons who perished, the millions whose sons returned. She raised no questions; no one suggested there were questions to raise. She hung out the stars; he put out the flag. And who was to help them do otherwise?

In her world, the modern world, war was like one of those public bouts between two brutes, an old-time-champ free for all. They stood toe to heel for fifty or more rounds, beating one another barefisted to death. The best the giants could expect was an interlude, a few minutes' recovery, water splashed on the bruised limbs, dazed eyes briefly focused. Then back to the mauling. Ding dong, next round.

The round named Vietnam spun my mother about, a weather vane in a tornado. She was now in her early seventies, entitled by every canon of the culture to a conventional fading, a sepia grandmother image, slipped between the pages of a Bible.

How we let go of them, the aged (how we let ourselves go)! To the attic, closed like a musty book, the trunk lid lowered, then off to the city dump. We deny them the grace of pain and freedom; we want them warehoused, disposed of. This is how we go, especially the men, those who survive the battlefields only to die, lumpish of mind and empty of eye, having paid their debt to biology and nothing at all to the fierce and sacrificial heart of reality.

She was denied that curse, that graceless ending. She was presented, at seventy, at eighty, with choices that burned in the hand like coals. Her sons heaped coals of fire and offered them; and she took them up and was burned to the bone.

Priests? Priests were conventional darlings of the nursery of heaven. Dolls, part of the cultural décor. Their powers, once formidable, were shrunken. Only here and there, among the young and the very old, were circles of belief; in them, priests could still shine. They forgave sins and comforted the ill and baptized infants. In sum, they were allowed to celebrate life, to mime it. All this, as long as they did not insist on living.

Her sons stepped down from that high, nearly foreclosed estate, two of us. We said our no as best we might, to the latest round of the bloody bout. We told her, gently as we might, of a fait accompli—our fate being, by then, all but determined by both church and state.

This was the great honor, the crown we put on her head, a crown of thorns. We did not want her to die, this unconventional, unbroken spirit, of a vapid moral decline, a melting of the ice, a fire that perished for want of fuel and air. We poked the fire, we breathed on her. And all this toward the end of her life, when she was weakened physically, when everything in the mad, frivolous culture would have her cosseted, cosmeticized, a corpse in a tufted box.

This was our gift to her, these last years. This is what draws the sting of regret or remorse. I know neither regret nor remorse toward her. What is there to regret? We offered her a place at the table of sacrifice, a place of honor, the honor due old age, no wasting game, no folderol of reverence.

She was ill. Philip was in prison. I was walking gingerly underground, shortly to be captured and shipped to prison. She was attended night and day by Jerry and Carol. These are the bare bones of that time. And we made it. All of us. No one perished, no one was harmed. No one of us, as far as we know, harmed others. Thus are the losses and gains of peacemaking totted up; in contrast, as may appear, to the losses and gains of war, which require no accounting here.

We came out of prison; there was a great reunion, then another and another. And eventually, in the course of nature, full of days and love, she died. No moral husk, but bursting like a pod with the seeds of eternity.

How describe that face, the face that bent over a first-born child, the face that turned to me in boyhood and manhood, that in her sublime, unrelenting old age, turned to me?

I was summoned from New York by the word, low-pitched with grief: "Come, she has just died."

With two brothers I entered her room. Her slight form had been arranged decently; bedclothing folded back, hands joined. Her jaws were toothless, face waxen, empty. The slate wiped clean; stillness, humiliation, mystery. We stood there, three of us, the clock of the universe stilled. We prayed a while; I bent over, kissed her cold forehead. Amen, alleluia.

SELF-PORTRAIT

I

According to a Hassidic story, a king once learned that the wheat harvest of his country was poisoned. Once eaten, the wheat would drive people mad.

The tragedy in fact occurred; no one who ate the wheat was spared. The kingdom endured a veritable plague of insanity.

The king sought in all his land for those few who had not eaten of the polluted crop. He summoned them, ordered them immediately to depart from the country. They were to dwell in foreign parts until allowed to return. In this way, the king told himself, at least a few would be spared the plague. And they would return, to remind the king and the people of the meaning of sanity.

What follows is a personal testimony.

I was released from federal prison in 1972, after serving nearly two years for resistance against the Vietnam war.

Since that time, my brother, friends, and I have tried to gain access to political leaders, to urge public debate on issues of nuclear arms, the new weaponry, the international arms trade. Always in vain. We kept at it, mindful of the advice of Gandhi that one must obey the law as long as is conscientiously possible. Finally we joined in a series of nonviolent civilly disobedient acts at the Pentagon and White House. We have also held nonviolent training sessions, spoken at countless churches and campuses, written extensively on the threat to human survival offered by the nuclear sword.

We have found to our dismay that the teaching of our church on nuclear war leaves most American Catholics untouched. That teaching is unequivocal and clear. But somewhere between Rome and the Atlantic Coast, the voice of Peter is deflected. On abortion, by way of contrast, the voice is deafening. But the question arises: Why children at all, if in ten or twenty years the world is reduced to ash?

In a dark hour, to remind myself of "the meaning of sanity," I compiled a pastiche of texts from the Vatican Council and the modern popes, from John through Paul, on nuclear arms. My "fifth gospel" goes something like this:

> The arms race is to be condemned unreservedly. . . . It is an injustice. . . . It is a form of theft. . . . It is an extremely grave affliction for humankind and does intolerable harm to the poor. . . . It is a scandal. . . . It is a mistake. . . . It is wrong, completely incompatible with the spirit of Christianity. . . . It is unthinkable that no other work can be found for hundreds of thousands of workers than the production of instruments of death. . . . It is a kind of hysteria, a folly based on fear, danger, and injustice. . . . It is meaningless, a means that does not achieve its end.

I also turn, these days, to the Book of Revelation. I name it fondly "The Nightmare of God." The nightmare is ourselves.

There I read (chapter 18) that an angel shouts "in a mighty voice, Babylon the great is fallen!"

This must be thought cold comfort. I am not afflicted with a death wish. But if the words are taken seriously, they seem to imply a mighty crisis in history. More, they announce that the utter ruin of the imperial venture is at hand. That venture implied cupidity, violence, collusion with merchants, money men, traders of the earth, kings and satraps. The mercantile society, consumed with appetite and possessions, is condemned, for it deals finally in "slaves, human souls."

We do not go to the Pentagon and White House to offer an "alternative policy," an "alternative politic," whatever that might mean. Our task is simply to proclaim the sin of mass destruction, the blasphemy against the God of life implied in weapons of mass killing. Only indirectly could this be called political activity.

We see such symbolic events as a proclamation, an announcement of gospel truth. A kind of passionate detachment governs our choice of occasion and symbol. We do not stand there to play God or to form a theater of cruelty or absurdity. Our acts are simply extensions of the sacraments (baptism, eucharist), celebrations of the liturgical year (Ash Wednesday, Good Friday, Easter, Holy Innocents).

We pour our own blood (and the media, in an immaculate mood, calls it "a red substance," or "red paint"). We scatter ashes of penance and destruction. We carry a large cross, printed with the names of the doomsday weaponry, the crucifixion of humanity. We dig graves, recalling the empty grave of Easter and the universal grave of nuclear intent.

In the sixties we were called crazy; in the seventies and eighties they say we are passé. Thus, the sixties are acceptable to the seventies, when the sixties are long past. Sixties, seventies, or eighties, history is a fast vehicle; but most take their readings through the rear-view mirror.

The tactics of those who live in a nonviolent tradition are indeed limited, from many points of view. In any case, the question of tactic is strictly secondary. Primary are soul, spirit, resource, the "unspeakable cries of the Holy Spirit" in us, even in us. Come Holy Spirit.

What do we have to offer the public scene in a dangerous time? After Three Mile Island, there is great stirring, action, resistance, outcry. It is a time of opportunity and crisis; and its dangers must be faced courageously, for the other side of such danger is a very explosion of conscience. And conscience alone can turn aside the cosmic blade.

Therefore, the crucial import of conduct that is disciplined and experienced and modest; the work of those who have charted the "other side" of the lunar American landscape.

It is clear to us, after thirty-five years of nuclear adventuring, that public authority is captive to Gog and Magog. But are we ourselves free? The question cannot be separated from readiness to face death in a good spirit.

Our culture has made the word *martyr* a tainted word; the word, we are told, implies self-righteousness, folly, ego. It assaults the pleasure principle; it blocks the way to the good life. Thus, we are robbed of a lode of extraordinary riches, a vein that, in other places, runs with pure and heroic blood. In Latin America, the walls of churches and homes bear the ikons of the holy ones, women and men of our lifetime; they have paid the supreme price for living the gospel in face of obscene tyranny.

But how terrible that, in our country, the military, the horrendous modern wars offer ikons of heroism. The rest of us die in our beds; our terminal disease is our culture.

At the Pentagon, and radiating outward across the land, is a vast, pulsing network of special interest, megacupidity, cost overruns, padding, economic piracy, dangerous and futile labor. The weapons are researched and built; but they bring their makers little of satisfied instinct, joy, professional pride. Meantime we lose the skills and services that are the patrimony of civilization itself; worse, vast numbers of professional people find themselves lost in the quagmire of the military, at the mercy of the next cold wind out of Vulcan's cave.

Thus is the abnormal constantly normalized. Thus, after a

generation of cold war, the abnormal is built into life itself, into public structure, into jobs, into conscience, into self-understanding. Violence is by now a kind of "second nature," in the classical sense. It is one with the Grand Canyon, Niagara Falls. Pilgrims visit the Pentagon exactly as they visit the natural spectaculars of our country; our artifacts, insolent, voracious, stand side by side with God's creation; blasphemy or blessing—who is to say?

And in the process, the abnormal is built into religion as well. There is by now a kind of brimstone piety at the heart of the Pentagon. The thousands of employees who require such a blessing are stroked by the clergy who serve there: "God is on our side."

Who this deity might be, who blesses devotees as they pursue their purpose of blowing up the world, remains unclear to many. Or perhaps it is all too clear.

The Book of Daniel speaks of the beast in the sanctuary. Perhaps today we must speak of the sanctuary in the beast.

While the abnormal is thus normalized, at runaway speed, aided and abetted by the major structures of society—while this goes on, nonviolent dissent is looked on with disdain and suspicion. "How abnormal!" is the cry.

There is a moral truth, as well as a psychological one, lurking here, if one can but come on it. A clue is the sentence of Huxley: "Technology may be defined as a faster way of going backward."

Indeed. As the right relation of means and ends is vitiated, as means are made more violent, precise, devouring, are declared virtuous or necessary or inevitable—at the same mad tempo, the purported ends ("peace, security, freedom") are polluted, defamed, ignored, violated in practice. To the point where, in sober fact, the means are in total control of the end; the end is a mad mix of impurity, deception and violence.

Nuclear blunders rush into this moral vacuum, threaten us

with overwhelming tragedy. The Harrisburg Syndrome is a shattering prelude. Its outcome is for the present by no means predictable, in the fate of the unborn, the ill, the aged, indeed all who live in the shadow of those monstrous stacks.

And then I reflect: dangers of nuclear power, desperate as they now appear, are but the tip of the nuclear blade.

But what is to become of us, of our children, of the earth itself, in view of the outpouring of nuclear weaponry? What disposition can we make, presuming we are somehow driven sane in years ahead, of our ten thousand nuclear warheads, our doomsday Trident submarine, our cruise missiles? We are sowing a whirlwind; who but we will reap it?

The forces that create this mad scenario also inoculate us against true knowledge and resistance. These forces are not technological or political at all; they are properly demonic. Christians, above all, may not ignore the spiritual dimensions of this horror, this death wish on rampage.

Which is to say, in a biblical sense, the Bomb has already detonated in our midst. Or, in a classical sense, the form precedes the fact; we must have imagined, internalized, been possessed by the Bomb, before we could consent to concoct it. This is perhaps why the Vatican Council condemned, not the detonation of such weapons, but their possession. The moral fallout is anomie, compulsive violence, glorification of blood and border, distraction from the truth of life. After years of this, we can scarcely call ourselves literate in the gospel. We read with dead eyes.

I have said for many years: We cannot have both the Bomb and the children. Until recently, such words were received with shrugs or downright anger. But no more.

The question is: Have we already chosen? (And not in favor of the children by any means.)

Glory be to God for all things. Even for the mad winds that drive us off too temperate a course, too lightly undertaken.

Now, like it or not, we must read the gospel in somewhat the same circumstances in which it was written: humiliation, public scorn.

II

In the summer of 1977, I celebrated a totally unexpected anniversary: my survival in the priesthood for twenty-five years and in the Jesuits for thirty-eight years. (I have heard a contrasting view from some quarters, suggesting that the church and the Jesuits have also survived me.) In any case, the occasion offered a good chance for some serious, joyful, even playful stock taking.

Questions like these arose in my mind: Are your symbols thriving? Are you still able to imagine the real world? Are your eyes seeing, your ears hearing, your heart beating—and this in a world that is largely dysfunctional, in a culture that lies there, terminally ill but still kicking?

I am on the whole happy to report a firm yes to such questions. One favorite way I have to demonstrate to my soul that I am alive, on the move, though rather deep in middle age, happy, cross-grained, angry, loving—is to reflect that, after some thirty-five years of writing poetry, I am still at it.

The poetry seems to me an index of vitality, close to the soul, a kind of sensor. So I would like to discuss a few poems, in a kind of running commentary. Through those I have chosen, I try to seize on and elaborate a number of crazy events (as well as a number of sane ones). Everything from the notorious exile, the law breaking, months underground, prison, the sixties and seventies (the eighties too, nothing finished with). Then, too, laborious, burdensome bread-and-butter survival, routine, the setbacks and moods, the rhythms of life pushing hard today.

Gratitude arises in me, inevitably: It is a kind of mystifying and constant angel. I am so grateful for the years of priesthood, the years among the Jesuits, my family and parents and friends. And for the poems, which seem equally undeserved. Poems like a kind of dark bulb of existence, a perennial root that, in spite of all, keeps coming on and up.

Gratitude is like a root pulled up at the end of summer; it

comes with a dark load of earth attached. Does one serve life best by cleaning the root off, or should I merely toss the root on the cellar floor, all its dirt and detritus attached? All that dark uncertainty, as well as a promise of something sinuous and seemly; even when the bulb lies there, dead to the world.

I think of the immediate past, where these years have taken me. I work in a cancer hospital in New York. I go periodically to the Pentagon, break the law, and am shunted on to court and into jail. I bounce about the country like a shuttlecock; with uncomprehending and dazed eyes, I gaze on great numbers of people. And I steal, like a con artist, those rare days when I get lost in order to reclaim a lost article, my own soul.

Meantime. With a Greek sense of the harsh necessity of things, I watch my country go down a foul drain of waste and want, of violence and anomie. I keep a kind of death watch on my church; a post-Vietnam postmortem soon to follow. I watch my beloved order, toe to toe with the culture in so many ways; many Jesuits mending cyclone fences, sporting mod clothing and hip language, talking psychobabble and corporate management and liberal politics.

I confess to being a part of all this. I am guilty of much of it; but I am trying to be less guilty. I honor, in this regard, Paul's admonition: "Be not conformed to this world." I like to translate the words in my own way: "Try to be as marginal as possible to madness."

Thus I work at the terminal hospital, St. Rose Home in New York, where I do what I can, hold the hands of the dying, serve them food and drink; more in fact than I can do for my dying country, my church, my order.

Again and again, I go to the Pentagon, where the stench of death is so severe as to shrivel the soul. There I chain myself to the doors like a vertical corpse (always with friends), pour blood and ashes, am dragged away—this time like a horizontal corpse. Thus things go.

I also write poetry; it is a method of submitting anger, horror, dread, faith, hope to a strict discipline. On the one hand, I do not want to live in the world without anger; on the other, I am not interested in dying just yet. But I do not want anger to burn useless as a waste flame from an oil stack. Living on, nursing my flame, I write. It is a way of surviving. It tells me my soul is my own. Indeed, that my soul is inalienable property, not to be trodden by mad tinkers and triflers, whether of the pentagonal or the twice-born variety (as often as not, the same variety).

Above all, I would like to be found faithful. I remember in this regard, the blank stares I once drew at a retreat in Ireland by declaring that "I had been searching for years for someone to be obedient to." That was a conservative statement, a profoundly traditional one, and so I meant it. For I am persuaded, in Simone Weil's phrase, that obedience is a need of the soul; that, without this proper scope and corrected shape and admonitory word, we languish and inflate and grow foolish, even to ourselves.

Indeed, what reason have I to trust myself or to walk in my own light? I have reason only to go in fear and trembling, a kind of vessel of darkness. Indeed, one has only to look abroad to see the catastrophic result of biblical disobedience, the loss of human measure and modesty. For some twelve years I saw my country grown blind beyond healing, violent beyond imagining, loosing Armageddon on a distant and inoffensive people, without reason, beyond any rule of law.

In so mad a time, I asked myself, was I to aid and abet my country? Was this the proper function of a Christian, a Jesuit? Or was I to resist my country? And if the latter, to whom could I go with my anger and torment? Who would say to me, "You must resist"? Who would say, "Break the iniquitous law; it is a chain on all our limbs"? Who would say, "Your direction is just; walk it; and I will walk with you"?

I hope that our no, the no of my brothers, my family, my friends, to the Vietnam war, and our continuing no to the nuclear-arms race—that this no is uttered within a larger yes. Saint Paul says simply in his letter to the Christians at Corinth that Jesus is the great yes of the Father. A yes to all creation and community, to all decency and candor, to all gentleness and courage, to the vast range of human charisms.

We cannot forget, though, that this yes was uttered in the days of His humiliation in the form of a bloody no to the powers of this world, to state and church alike. A no that earned for Him the prompt verdict of capital punishment.

I would like to be found faithful. I have a poem to offer on this theme. The poem should not, I think, require much preliminary tutoring, for it means to say something quite simple. Whenever a government, even a revolutionary one, gets established, I know in my bones that I've become an outsider once more. I long, in some ideal order of things, to be friend and advocate of every new youngster on the block (so to speak)—especially to befriend any who get worked over by a neighborhood bully named Sam. But the speed with which the new arrival learns the methods of the bully never ceases to appall me. In such circumstances, I turn away both from bully and quondam bullied; toward other ways, peoples, clues.

So the poem turns from the international scene (a conventicle of bullies if ever there was one) and lingers around an old man and his dying wife, who together kept a store on my street in New York.

FIDELITY

Coming up Broadway, a fruitless evening
reception at U.N., the "revolutionary ambassador"
resounding like a stale ash tray or like
the secretary of any state you mention & reflecting

sadly, the old game starts again
before the bloody flag is hoisted dry.
Life's an Orson Welles turn out of Graham Greene;

    The train rushes on, our hero in fatigues
        saunters down the careening aisle
        of the third class carriage
        expansive, macho
        he disappears into mirrors

    Minutes later he stands there—
    diplomat's stripes, strictly first class
    stiff as a sword cane. He's hardened, molten to mirror.

Alas folks, freaks, minority spirits, we've lost again.
It rains on Broadway, tears of knowledge.
I look for a store to buy a pen to blacken, blear
a page, tears or rain. I'll walk to 104th Street

where my old friend the picture framer
propped a photo of his dead wife in the window.

> Rain worsens
> Knowledge goes under

He was inefficient and faithful
she, propped in a wheelchair like a cauliflower
in a stall, months and months. Every hour or so

> lit a cigarette
> put it to her lips;
> One day
> a crazy old black woman
> named by me, Crazy Horse
> came by
> leaned convivially over

the speechless mindless creature, yelled
"How are you dearie?" and kissed her like a luv.

I've long pondered fidelity. You can't know
even Gerald Ford that lethal dummy, might be snatched
from mad comics by his cancerous wife.

When the old woman
grew hopelessly ill, he closed the cramped
musty curiosity shop at 2 PM each day, took a taxi

> to Misericordia Hospital,
> sat there at bedside
> all evening. One day
> slight good news;
> "She ate something, they've

stopped the intravenous feeding." A merciful interlude only;
  she died that night in his arms. On this foul foot path
  mule track, death mile, oblivion alley, bloody pass
  Broadway, pith and paradigm of the world, cutting the
  50 states of amnesia like a poisoned pie; a swollen Styx

an Augean drain ditch

      a lotus blooms.

He looked up grey faced as I came in. "She went peacefully
your green plant was a comfort." Still, wishing I could summon

for myself, for my friends, someday

           for the world at large—
           yes the self damned
           the hypocrites, the power brokers
           the "revolutionary ambassadors"

           a bare whiff of that bloom

hand laid on hand signifying a sacrament.

           When I edged in sideways
           past the morose dying
           woman, her wheelchair
           lodged like an embolism
           in the body politic,
           her skin
           wrapped like a rodent's
           in a moth eaten muff
           I came
           not off magical Broadway
           into Ripoff Boutique
           but where
           springs have source

stream meeting stream signifying a sacrament.

*   *   *

Inevitably, the question of Jesus arises, the question of faith
in Him. Looking back over the years of my life, a strange fact
emerges. I cannot discover when (or even whether) He first
entered my life. Was there indeed such an occasion or point of
time? I am inclined to doubt it. Jesus was a gift, given me by my
parents, as to them by theirs; through time, we had simply put
on Jesus with the flesh and bones of our race, had taken him in
with our mother's milk. There was no conscious point at which
we met Him. He was consubstantial with us, in the clumsy,

old-fashioned phrase. How precious that truth is to me! Jesus, a reality both immanent and majestic, a dweller in the bloodline, indeed the very blood of that blood, as well as the One seated in the clouds of heaven.

Still, the facts of life intrude, go slow.

Since 1970, I have been in the following circumstances: underground, fleeing the law, in and out of jail repeatedly. Many have been out of countenance with me: some announcing the will of Jesus, some speaking for Caesar. While underground I had written a book; its theme came from my reading of Saint John of the Cross. I named the book *The Dark Night of Resistance.* I confess in the book to a kind of double sense of Jesus; on the one hand I was instructed from my earliest years in the teachings of Christ. And yet—and yet, I had a haunting sense of being betrayed.

My fitful and nightmarish life had finally exposed the betrayal, a false supposition about Jesus, a supposition as powerful as it was universal. Namely, that true knowledge of Jesus could be separated from experience of the cross.

Now I had to question this. Could I come to a vital, adult sense of Christ without having my life literally blown apart? Could I tread the old track in the old cassock (or indeed, in the new, mod, chic duds) and still hold in my heart anything but an illusion of Christ?

It occurred to me that, if I were to pursue the question honestly, I would be required to start over, to retrace my steps.

And in the midst of these ponderings, something else struck me with the brutal force of lightning. The induction of Jesus into our worldliness, our armies, our fascism and violence, had not only betrayed me, in a sense it undid Him as well. He was bound hand and foot in the toils of our hideous story, Prometheus in chains. Western history was not only hostile to my search for a right religious sense, to truthful images of Christ. It had also betrayed, immobilized Christ. Could He see His face in the mirror of our hypocritical worship, our big claims and puny amoral performance? Could He recognize Himself in such robes as were thrust on Him by Constantinian arrangements, so often renewed? Christ of the battlefield, Christ of the colonizers, Christ of the consumers, Christ of the racists, Christ of Roman diplomacy, Christ of the White House masses and Pentagon prayer rooms, Christ of tax-exempt properties, Christ of the military chaplains and the executive prayer sessions?

What had we done to Him? We had broken Him on the mad wheel of the world.

This was my poetic conceit (and something more). I saw my life (His life?) as a recessive journey, a voyage to the sources. He and I together would step back and back, into a kind of fetal darkness, reduced to a mere egg, a cellular speck. And thereupon, I would recover something of that life, that presence so nearly an absence, that all so near nothing.

A new beginning, a making new. The poem that came of all this, as the reader will discover to his dismay (this being the sole poem in my repertory that once, at a reading, occasioned a walkout), is simply nightmarish. And as its logo, prologue, motto, I offer the following:

> Given the god (gods, God, Gods, the nomenclature and number is unclear) of most of us, Christ must be an argument against God's existence. Given the Christ of most of us, the real Christ must be dumb as an unhatched egg.

> Given the leap of the Gerasene swine over the brink, the only command likely to be of help to humans, is that implied in the poem: Step Back!

To Christ Our Lord

To believe
you have to disbelieve
unstitching like love's sweet
cheat, the day's meticulous rainbow

But these, jackals
on the spoor of jackals
eat you like dead bees
for lust of the honeycomb
scatter you, death's parade.

Then priests wheel in like bears on unicycles
overtrained, underpaid
like motorized brooms they love debris
their vocation;
     bees' husks, taffeta remnants
confetti, all that's left
of the dead parade

O golden goose named Pharaoh
     they made you glorious
       only for their kitchen—
  for lust of that savory
    paté ROMANITÀ

       Roman goose
guardian of San Angelo
    honking the devils off the sacred
         precincts
   we found you dead & scattered
     for lust of a golden egg
       no sooner born
than, closed, clouded like an eye

    You brood there in the dark
       like your own egg
   you glimmer there in the dark like a
        world ransoming pearl—

    like a petrified tree
          your heart of stone
        your gospel a stone
   you
an argument against God's existence
And the jackals chorus—
    if he were not if he were not

Unto myself then! I step back back back

   what is done is undone
     what is believed is disbelieved

      I whisper
    like the first day of winter
      disbelieve!

and close my eyes
like a wintry animal
and stop my heart in its shroud
and forbid life, and life giving metaphors.

*   *   *

On to the third poem. A dark nimbus surrounds it; but it is also incontinently playful.

I once saw, portrayed in a transept window of Chartres Cathedral, four evangelists mounted on the shoulders of four prophets. The conception was breathtaking: stark, primitive, a balancing act. The one below takes the weight; the one above sees further, must tell what he sees, must use all that borrowed strength and height to form a wider vision.

As I reflected on the image, it became a kind of circus act. As though the two, prophet and evangelist, stood there on a high wire, part of the great show of creation that we call the church. There, the action is death defying, animals and people are in concert and conflict. There freaks are on view. There the drab routine of life in the world is relieved and refreshed and shaken up. There indeed (this goes for the best circuses) no one does merely one thing; but roles and costumes are interchanged; all sorts of menial and skilled people do all sorts of skilled and menial things under the central pole in the vast, airy tent.

There is another image in the poem. The old voyagers used to speak of sailing by the stars. The method seems to have worked rather well. It required, of course, a detailed knowledge of those celestial orbs, more accurate by far than the sketchy geography of the earth's surface then available. More to the point of the poem, the stars crowded the heavens with a populous glory: heroes, demigods, and goddesses shed on the earth a very epiphany, a promise, a radiant possibility of beatitude. At least one of these stars, we are told, stood firm, while the other creatures and creators danced about it. The North Star.

I thought that a neat fact and metaphor. The North Star gave point, a center, to the action above, even while it gave direction, means, end to the action below; this corresponded quite neatly to the double universe spoken of by the Greeks and borrowed

for other purposes by the author of the Letter to the Hebrews
and the Book of Revelation.

In any case, enough prose. Here is the poem.

O Catholic Church

I could love you more if
you mothered me less, if you
egged on like a shrew by expensive shrinks
and your own shrinking shadow
weren't such an
Amazon of Order

Let me tell you my dream; a
circus act. I'm performing
under the tent's navel, swinging out
over and over, hundreds of feet up;
one half million eyes down there

can't believe the act. And you're the
anchor rope, the
lynch pin, the
center pole

No; better, it's
your act and mine!
skills, courage perfectly mutual—
tonight you're on my shoulders;
the long horizontal pole vibrates with the subdued
energy, passion, anguish of the world;
north pole to south
horrendous, exultant news passing through
your hands and mine—
and we move
and we move it
and we are moved

One body, vertical, functional, ecstatic—
a figure of the future?
a window of Chartres Cathedral
evangelists on the shoulders of prophets
two freedoms making a less imperfect freedom

Then sometimes I dream you're the North Star.

And (this is no dream)
though I am forced to eat papier maché for breakfast
and fret for the death of my friends
served up like cat and dog food
to alley cats, to mad dogs—
noble souls whose only offense is
they resist the recycling of kangaroos into
the elegant eclair shit of
Park Avenue pimps

Still dear friend, if
you are the North Star
please say so now and then;
not incessantly
not with a Xerox blizzard from outer space
no, only a word
from a starry mouth
heard softly here and there
with authority too

—a forefinger pointing
—a voice saying "north"

We could infer the other directions;
south, east, west; and their
finer divisions, down to the hairlines

But bickering, wandering, not knowing
Do not from *doughnut,* north from south—
this is our madness!

And you could relieve it!

Pope John, from northern Italy, once helped.

III

September 27, 1980, marked my first visit to the monastery
at Gethsemane, Kentucky, since the death of Merton in 1968.
I was asked to offer the homily at morning mass; the text was
from Matthew for the feast of Saint Vincent de Paul.

> I bless you, Father of heaven and earth, for hiding these
> things from the learned and clever, and revealing them to the
> children . . .

And Matthew continues, with unexampled solemnity more typical of John:

> . . . No one knows the Son except the Father, just as no one
> knows the Father except the Son—and those to whom the Son
> chooses to reveal Him.

Then a glance descends; face to human face, He takes us in:

> Come to me all you who labor and are burdened, and I will
> give you peace. Take up my yoke, learn of me; I am meek and
> humble of heart. You will find rest for your souls, for my yoke
> is easy, my burden light.

In Jesus we learn of the modesty of God.

I set this down in a time of Promethean muscle building,
muscling in, a time of no limits, a time when literally everything
is allowed: genetic splicing, abortions on demand, nuclear warheads pocking the landscape. We learn too well the sad litany
of human excess: the last national political campaign, for example, in which the nuclear-arms race is simply not an issue; the
only question being: How much more how quickly? Death always inflicted elsewhere, the artificers of death presumably safe
and sound in a nuclear free fire zone. We are gently driven mad.

The modesty of God.

After mass, we visited Merton's grave. Nearby a fresh mound
arose. I was told of a brother recently deceased: "We buried
him in his red socks. He was a kind of Santa Claus in the community."

Among Trappists there is no embalming, no casket or outer
box. A brother descends into the grave, receives the body as it
is lowered. He covers the face with a cowl, the earth is shoveled
in.

But Merton was buried in a box, his body shipped half across
the world, most of the journey in an Air Force plane.

We trudged up the hill to the cottage where Merton spent his last years. Some sat about in the suave autumn sunlight on the porch facing the valley. Bob Lax began reading from Tom's poetry, *Cables to the Ace.*

I went walking in the woods, the paths he and I had taken fifteen years before. How different the little dwelling appeared, as though time had spun it around, the pivot of those hills. And the trees; where we once sat facing an empty field, unfolding away and away like a sea swell, now mature trees cast up their spume or flame. And around us a ten-foot crest of hedge blew and blew.

This is what Merton wrote me in August 1964:

> I realize that I am at the end of some line. What line? What is the trolley I am probably getting off? The trolley is called a special kind of hope . . . of things getting more intelligible . . . being set in a new kind of order and so on.
> Point one, things are not going to get better.
> Point two, things are going to get worse.
> I will not dwell on point two.
> Point three, I don't need to be on the trolley anyway.
> You can call the trolley anything you like, I have gotten off it.
> You can call the trolley a form of religious leprosy if you like. It is burning out. In a lot of sweat and pain if you like, but it is burning out for real . . . that leprosy of temporal hope, that special expectation that young monks have, that priests have. As a priest I am a burnt out case . . .
> So burnt out that the question of standing up and so forth, becomes irrelevant. I just continue to stand there where I was hit by the bullet.
> And I will continue standing there . . .
> But I have been shot dead, the situation is different. I have no priestly ax to grind with anyone about anything . . .
> The funny thing is that I will probably continue to write books. And word will go around about how they got this priest who was shot, and they got him stuffed, sitting up at a desk, propped up with books and writing books; this book machine that was killed. I am waiting to fall over; it may take about ten

more years. When I fall over it will be a big laugh because I
wasn't there at all . . .
I am sick to the teeth . . . with explanations about where we
are all going, because where we are all going is where we went
a long time ago, over the falls. We are in a new river and we
don't know it . . .

He wrote of having ten years, but he had only four. Then he fell
over.

To be alive to the future one had best poke about in the past,
at least now and then. I went to the monastery to seek a measure
of light on why I had gone, some weeks before, to King of
Prussia, Pennsylvania. And there, in the words of our statement,

. . . beat swords into plowshares . . . exposed the criminality
of nuclear weaponry and corporate piracy. . . . We commit
civil disobedience at General Electric because this genocidal
entity is the fifth leading producer of weaponry in the U.S. To
maintain this position, G.E. drains $3 million a day from the
public treasury, an enormous larceny against the poor.
We wish also to challenge the lethal lie spun by G.E. through
its motto, "We bring good things to life." As manufacturers
of the Mark 12A reentry vehicle, G.E. actually prepares to
bring good things to death. Through the Mark 12A, the threat
of first-strike nuclear war grows more imminent. Thus G.E.
advances the possible destruction of millions of innocent
lives.

If a plumb line could lie horizontal, in time rather than space,
then the line, tight as a bowstring, would lie between the monastery and General Electric. I do not know how to put matters
more simply. Somewhere along that line we stand (if we are
lucky; it is literally a lifeline). We touch it; the line is not dead
at all, inert. It vibrates with the message of a living universe. At
one end, a monastery, a hive of stillness and listening and
strength. And at the other, an unspeakable horror, a factory of
genocide.

To taste death and life, you go to headquarters; you listen and
learn from the experts.

No sylvan setting for General Electric, no fooling around. Austerity, efficiency, cost value, big bang for big buck. You drive into an industrial park, down a broad macadam highway: building after building, anonymous, wall-eyed, abstract. A campus of world experts in the science and practice of abstract death.

September 9.

We rose at dawn after (to speak for myself) a mostly sleepless night. In and out of dream, in and out of nightmare. The refrain was part nuptial chant, part dirge; the latter theme dominant, the former a minor key indeed. Brasses, kettle drums, and now and again the plaintive flute in obligato, the cry of an infant in the river reeds.

We had passed several days in prayer together, an old custom indeed, as old as our first arrests in the late sixties. We were mostly vets of those years, survivors too; survivors of the culture and its pseudos and counters, survivors of courts and jails, of the American flare of conscience and its long hibernation, survivors in our religious communities, in our families (they having survived us!). By an act of God and nothing of our own, survivors of America—its mimes, grimaces, enticements, abhorrences, shifts and feints, masks, countermasks. Survivors (barely) of the demons who, challenged, shouted their name: Legion!

We knew for a fact (the fact was there for anyone who bothered to investigate) that General Electric in King of Prussia manufactures the reentry cones of Mark 12A missiles. We learned that Mark 12A is a warhead that will carry an H-bomb of 335 kilotons to its target. That three of these weapons are being attached to each of three hundred Minuteman III missiles. That because of Mark 12A accuracy and explosive power, it will be used to implement United States counterforce or first-strike policy.

We knew these hideous cones (*shrouds* is the G.E. word) were concocted in a certain building of the G.E. complex. The building is huge; we had no idea exactly where the cones could be found.

Of one thing we were sure: If we were to reach the highly classified area of shipping and delivery, and were to do there what we purposed, Someone must intervene, give us a lead.

After our deed, a clamor arose among the FBI and state and county and G.E. (and God knows what other) police who swarmed into the building.

"Did they have inside information? Was there a leak?"

Our answer: Of course we had inside information; of course there had been a leak. Our informant is otherwise known in the New Testament as Advocate, Friend, Spirit. We had been at prayer for days.

And the deed was done. We eight looked at one another, exhausted, bedazzled with the ease of it all. We had been led in about two minutes, and with no interference to speak of, to the heart of the labyrinth.

They rounded us up, trundled us out in closed vans. We spent the day, uncommonly cheerful in that place of penitence, in various cells of the police headquarters. We underwent what I came to think of as a "forced fast," the opposite of forced feeding, and undoubtedly less perilous to life and limb. Around the corridors of the spiffy new building (we were in G.E. country, the economy is forty percent G.E.; G.E. brings good things to life) the atmosphere was one of hit and miss, cross-purpose, barely concealed panic. How the hell did they get into the building so easily? How about our jobs, we who were purportedly guarding the nuclear brews and potions?

Lines to Justice Department, Pentagon, FBI were red-hot. Why can't you get your act together up there? And what are we to do with these religious doomsayers? Let them go, let them off light, let them off never? Please advise!

About noon another ploy got under way. They loaded us in vans again; back to the scene of the crime. It was like a Mack Sennett film played backward; first you were sped away in a black Maria, then you were backed freakishly into the same doorway. (It devolved later that they wanted identification by the employees.)

But they wouldn't talk, so we wouldn't walk.

They carried four or five of us out of the van—into that big warehouse room, the bloody floor, the bloody, torn blueprints stamped "top secret." And then the missile cones, broken, bloodied, useless. No more genocide in our name! And the wall of faces, police, employees, silent as the grave, furious, bewildered, a captive nation.

Under shrill orders From Somewhere, the charade was halted. The procedure was illegal. A district attorney said it might endanger their whole case. Indeed.

So back to durance vile. They locked us up; they kept saying: Sure we'll feed you, presently we'll charge you. And nothing happened.

By five P.M. the more inventive among us were ready to close their eyes, strip their shoe laces, and pretend we were eating spaghetti Rossi in the West Village.

Then something happened. One by one we were led out. Take off your shoes. And (to the six males) take off your pants.

It appeared that, these objects being stained with our blood, they were severely required as evidence.

So like the bad, little boys in the fairy tale, supperless and shoeless, we were led off to our destiny by Stepmother State.

An institution that we and others have been pondering for a long time, grows on us, presses closer.

To wit: In a time of truly massive irrationality, one had best stop playing the old academic-ecclesial game of Scrabble, as though merely putting words together could make sense of moral incoherence, treachery, meandering apathy—could break that spell.

Rationality? Reason? If these were ever in command, they had certainly fled the scene during the Vietnam war. I would be willing to venture that sanity, reason, have never sat in the catbird seat again.

In the saddle of power and decision we have, instead, a kind of "Eichmania" analyzed by Merton: a tightly hierarchical, spiritually captivated, ideologically closed insanity. In it are caught the multicorporations and their squads of engineers and planners, on and up to the highest responsible chairs of command—the Pentagon and White House. All, so to speak (so to doublespeak), "bring good things to life."

And then outward into society, the malaise touches all with a leprous finger; meandering apathy, at least as complex an illness as rotten power. Apathy, the natural outcome of such authority, so used.

We have evidence of such indifference to moral and physical disaster in other modern societies—societies whose citizens, under whip and lash, or under a rain of bread and politics of the circus, stood helpless, helpless to win the nod of blind, deaf fate, to speak up, to force a hearing.

Such apathy shows face today in our inability to summon resistance against nuclear annihilation. Screen out the horror; a shutter comes down. Best not to imagine what might be; best to act as though the worst could not be.

The phenomenon before the catastrophe is remarkably like the phenomenon after the catastrophe. Many of the survivors of Hiroshima, afflicted with radiation sickness, conceal their illness as long as possible, "act as though" they had not been stricken. They go so far as to falsify family history, conceal the fact that they were in the orbit of death on the day of the bomb.

No wonder that today Americans find it more plausible, more conducive to sanity, to ignore our nuclear plight, to fight for survival in areas where the facts are less horrid, the cards less stacked. Economic woes, job layoffs, inflation—we have enough trouble drawing the next breath. And you with your little hammers and bottles of blood go out against Goliath? Thanks, good luck. But no, thank you.

Blood and hammers. The symbolic aspect of our G.E. action has appealed to some and appalled others. But almost no one who has heard of the action lacks an opinion about it, usually a passionately stated one.

In pondering these passions, so long dormant, newly released, one learns a great deal—not about passions in a void, but about vital capacities for survival, socibility, soul.

Some who hear grow furious; some of the furious are Catholics; Catholics also guard us, judge us, prosecute us. This is an old story, which need not long detain us.

What is of peculiar and serious interest here is the use and misuse of symbols, their seizure by secular power; then the struggle to keep the symbols in focus, to enable them to be seen, heard, tasted, smelled, lived and died for, in all their integrity, first intent.

Their misuse. How they are leveled off, made consistent with the credo of the state. Thus, to speak of King of Prussia, and our symbol there: blood. Its outpouring in the death of Christ announced a gift and, by implication, set a strict boundary, a taboo. No shedding of blood, by anyone, under any circumstances, since "this, My blood, is given for you." Blood as gift.

Hence the command: No killing, no war. Which is to say, above all, no nuclear weapons. And thence the imperative: Resist those who research, deploy, or justify, on whatever grounds, such weaponry.

Thus the drama; the symbol outpoured implies a command. Do this; so live, so die. Clear lines are drawn for public as well as personal conduct. Church and state, the "twin powers," always in danger of becoming Siamese twins, are in fact kept from a mutually destructive symbiosis by imperative and taboo. More, they are revealed for what they in fact are: radically opposed spiritual powers, as in chapter 13 of Revelation. Church can never be state; state is forbidden to ape or absorb church. And this mutual opposition, this nonalignment, this friction and fraying, erupts from time to time in tragic and bloody struggle. The church resists being recast as Caesarian ikon. The state, robust, in firm possession, demands that the church knuckle under, bend knee, bless war, pay taxes, shut up. Church, thy name is trouble.

The choices are not large. Toil and trouble or—capitulation. In the latter case, all is lost. The symbols are seized at the altar and borne away. Now the blood of Christ, the blood of humans, is cheap indeed; for what could be cheaper than blood the church itself has declared expendable? That blood is now a commodity, a waste. When Caesar speaks, blood may be shed at will—by Christians or others, it makes no difference. Which is also to say, there exists no longer any distinction in fact between armed combatants and citizens, between soldiers and little children. Killing has become the ordinary civil method of furthering civic ends. The sacred symbol of blood, whose gift urged the command (thou shalt not kill)—that blood is admixed, diluted, poisoned. It is lost in a secular vortex, immensely vigorous and seductive, urging a different vision. Labor is commodity, the flag is a sacred *vexillum*, humans are productive integers, triage rules the outcome. Finally, a preemptory secular command: Thou shall kill when so ordered—or else.

It seems to me that since Hiroshima, to set an arbitrary moment, this debasing of the sacred symbols into secular use and misuse has proceeded apace.

To undo the blasphemy, what a labor!

We have been at this for years—dramatic events, deliberately orchestrated, arbitrary but intensely traditional, liturgical, illegal, in every case wrenching the actors out of routine and community life—to face the music, face the public, face the jury.

Is it all worth it? In measure, the eight who acted at King of Prussia have already answered the question. At least for themselves, and for one another. One of them said in the course of our discussion: "Even if the action went nowhere, if no one understood or followed through on it, I would still go ahead."

Worth it for ourselves. Each of us had, before the act, to plumb our motives, consult loved ones, care for the future of children, arrange professional and community responsibilities, measure, in fact, all good things against this "one necessary thing." And decide.

The eight so decided: Yes. Such an act must be taken, even though it will disrupt almost everything else, call many things in question, inflict suffering on others. The value of the act is thus measured by the sacrifice required in order to do it; an old and honored Christian idea, if I am not mistaken.

(For us, going as we did in fear and trembling, from the eucharist to General Electric, September 9 had the feel of the last hours of Jesus: His journey from the upper room to death. We held our liturgy the night before, broke the bread, passed the cup. Light of head, heavy of heart, we nonetheless celebrated by anticipation the chancy event of the following day, and the trial to come, and the penalty. Our logic? The Body was "broken for you"; the cup "poured out for all."

(The logic was not only our own. At one court hearing, the prosecutor asked, with more than a show of contempt, under prodding from his chief, who referred to me as "this so-called priest" and "this wandering gypsy" [sic], "And when did you last celebrate mass?" I was obviously to be shown up as not only rootless, but faithless as well.)

But what of the larger meaning of the action: its value for the church and the public?

Here one must go slow. The value of the act for those who propose it, sweat it out, do it—this is more easily determined. Value is created, so to speak, in the breach, in a decision to gather, to unite voices in an outcry, to precipitate a crisis that, at least for a time, will strip away the mask of evil.

But I know of no sure way of predicting where things will go from there, whether others will hear and respond, or how quickly or slowly. Or whether the act will fail to vitalize others, will come to a grinding halt then and there, its actors stigmatized or dismissed as fools. One swallows dry and takes a chance.

There was one sign that our action touched a nerve. A hasty attempt was made on the day of the action itself to discredit us through a dizzying list of charges. Ideology, panic, special interests combined to barrage the media and the public with a verdict before the verdict: Mere violent crazies had gone on a rampage. The charges included assault, false imprisonment, reckless endangerment, criminal mischief, terroristic threats, harassment, criminal coercion, unlawful restraint. Talk about overkill! We sat in court, transfixed, gazing on our images in the crazy mirrors of the state fun house.

It takes a measure of good sense to stand firm at such moments. People gifted with our nefarious history must remind themselves that at King of Prussia, hammers and blood in hand, we set in motion a lengthy and complex drama. One should speak perhaps of three acts.

The first act belonged in the main to us: an early-morning curtain raiser, the action under way. In a sense, the adversaries have not yet appeared; only a few subalterns act: on their behalf, in their name: the guards and police and employees. But G.E. has not yet turned on its voltage. No official appears in justifying garb to bespeak the ancient myths, to invoke sacrosecular outrage at the violation of a holy place, property off bounds, the shrine accessible only to initiates. (Antigone has buried her brother's body; but Creon has not yet flogged his way to condemn her.)

Then a second act opens. It marks the marshaling of forces of law and order, the invoking of the daemons of natural law, secular karma. Anger, retaliation are in the air; the gods of property buzz furious overhead. The actors all but tear up the script of act one; an assault is mounted on the earlier reliance on "higher law" or "conscience." Behold true conscience, behold the highest law of all, the law by which all citizens must live, the law that is our common safeguard against anarchy!

So in the manner of Shakespeare or Pirandello or Sophocles, act two is a kind of play within the play. The audience is bewildered, thrown off guard. It had read a certain kind of admirable moral truth in the face of the young woman Antigone (in the faces of a nun, of the mother of six, of a lawyer, of a professor, of a seminary graduate—faces like credentials of moral worth), now it hears another kind of truth. This is not the truth of "symbolic action," which from a legal point of view is always murky, easily discredited, and reaching troublesomely as it does into dark existence (the forbidden burial of a brother, the breaking and bloodying of ikons) must be exorcised, discredited by measured, relentless argument.

The argument, of devastating force, in ancient Greece as today, I call that of the Great If.

The example of Antigone, the example of the eight, is deliberately magnified, made stark. Behold their act, performed under clerical guise, under the guise of virtue. Behold their act, as viewed by the state, the guardian and interpreter of public morality. (What an unconscious and ironic tribute is paid the defendants here, as though in the court itself the state were erecting, stone by stone, a monument to the conscience it so fears—and so magnifies.)

In any case, citizens and believers, whatever divagations of spirit they were beckoned toward by the conduct of the protagonists, by their age or condition or credentials (above all, by their dark, probing symbols)—all this is brought up, short and abrupt. You are in court, this audience as extensions of the jury, who are in effect extensions of the judge. You are here not to indulge in murky existential probings, but to consider the letter of the law, and in your hearts, to approach a verdict.

Finally, act three. Many scenes and changes: the great world, a time between events (action/trial) the agora, the courtroom, the many places where people discuss, argue, make up their minds and unmake them again, slowly or with speed come to a conclusion, the knotting of the action.

In court, the argument of the Great If is relentlessly pursued. The crime of the eight is segregated from the world; the faces of the defendants, mirrors of conscience, are hooded. The inert symbols—hammers, empty, bloodied bottles—lie there, tagged, soulless, mere items of evidence. They are relics of moral defeat, emblems of legal punishment; as such, the prosecutor will refer to them with disdain and handle them with distaste. They will be compared, subtly or openly, to the tools of safe crackers, bloodied knives, guns. In any case: What If such implements became the common tools of so-called conscience? What If all citizens, under whatever itch for notoriety, took up such tools? (Like the soiled hands of Antigone, heaping foul dust on her brother's body, against the law of the state—how sordid a venture!)

In the course of this act, the classic Greek formula is verified: the purging of pity and fear.

These must be purged. For pity and terror get in the way of spiritual change. They are obstructive emotions, to be taken seriously, no doubt, but strictly as preliminary to the main event.

That event, in a large sense, is destined to occur neither on stage nor in the court. It is rather the unending, passionate pursuit of moral good, the righting of injustice, the ousting of death, the reordering of an ethical universe and of its social and political forms.

But in order to be purged, pity and fear have first to be aroused.

How acute the Greeks were! In the first days following our action, friends invariably spoke of their forebodings: their dread of the harsh sentences that undoubtedly would befall us, their fear that our action would be ignored or misconstrued.

Pity and fear. The pity narrows emotional largesse; the fear spreads out inordinately, claims all minds. Fear of the future, fear for children bereft of parents, fear of the state and its legal savageries.

One emotion is too narrow, the other too diffused. Neither finally is useful; that is to say, neither serves to heighten the truth, the universal predicament (which is not defined by prison sentences, but by nuclear annihilation)—or to grant hints and leads as to a way out.

I must inject here a message from the jails of Pennsylvania. If the eight have insisted on anything, it is that their trial and imprisonment are not the issue at stake. Pity for them gains nothing. Neither does fear for them, or for their children and spouses. The eight go their way, a way meticulously chosen and after much prayer. But the issue they raise will continue to shadow lives and vex hearts. It is the corporate crimes of General Electric, the race toward oblivion that this monstrous entity both fuels and illustrates.

Finally, what drove us to "such extremes"?

To reach the truth, one must turn from Creon to Antigone, from the prosecutor, in our case, to the gospel.

In America, in 1980, it could hardly be called useful to the common weal, or a mitigation of the common woe, that a group of religious folk enter a megadeath factory—in vain proof that they are in possession of some kind of magical counterforce.

Why then?

Let us say merely, because they hungered for the truth, for its embodiment, longed to offer a response to its claim on us. That even through us, an all-but-submerged voice might be heard—voice of "God, not of the dead, but of the living."

From our statement: "In confronting G.E., we choose to obey God's law of life, rather than a corporate summons to death. Our beating of swords into plowshares is a way to enflesh this biblical call. In our action, we draw on a deep-rooted faith in Christ, who changed the course of history through his willingness to suffer rather than to kill. We are filled with hope for our world and for our children as we join this act of resistance."

IV SEQUEL

Dearest friends—all who stood with us, walked with us, burned incriminating documents with us, endured the legal farce with us; also prepared food and lodging, answered phones, swept floors etcetera etcetera—

The illustration right says very nearly everything. It was a kind of Stonehenge moment in the mind. Advisory lawyers doing a walkout, eight of us standing with backs to the judge; one by one, the audience rising and doing likewise. A solid wall of wills, a stupendous silent no to the absurd puppetry.

We were convicted on three charges; the occurrence has hit the authorities with an absolutely delicious irony. They are now free to remand us to their dungeons, whence they have recently and summarily ejected four of us. Or they can slap us on the wrist with time served.

Now if you don't particularly want someone taking your jail apart, and if you don't want them making more complex the functions of your industrialmilitary complex—then what do you do?

We await sentencing. A pallid phrase indeed in face of our passionate intent to continue resisting the machinery of mega-death. I am traveling the country, writing, meeting with our *kairos* group. We are preparing yet another action at Riverside Research, that cave of bent minds, intent on (I swear) the theory and practice of laser-beam warfare. We will vigil and pray and some of us will be arrested on the Friday we name Good.*

Please remember at prayer our sisters and brothers of like actions, those in jail in California and Texas and elsewhere.

May Easter summon us forth with a trumpet blast, from tombs of dread and inertia. Tombs blocked at mouth with—missiles. Come, mighty angel, roll them back!

♡ Daniel

* 12 arrested, court dates in May.